Bush's Secret World

Bush's Secret World

Religion, Big Business and Hidden Networks

Eric Laurent

Translated by Andrew Brown

polity

Ouvrage publié avec le concours du ministère français chargé de la Culture – Centre national du livre.
Published with the assistance of the French Ministry of Culture – National Centre for the Book.

First published in 2004 by Polity Press

Polity Press
65 Bridge Street
Cambridge CB2 1UR, UK

Polity Press
350 Main Street
Malden, MA 02148, USA

ISBN: 0-7456-3348-X
ISBN: 0-7456-3349-8 (pb)

A catalogure record for this book is available from the British Library and has been applied for from the Library of Congress.

Typeset in 11 on 13 pt Berling
by SNP Best-set Typesetter Ltd., Hong Kong
Printed and bound in Great Britain by MPG Books, Bodmin, Cornwall

For further information on Polity, visit our website: www.polity.co.uk

Contents

1

Towards Apocalypse

In November 2000 George W. Bush became the forty-third President of the United States, after the most controversial and muddled election in the whole of American political history. In fact, he was elected despite winning 337,576 votes fewer than his Democratic adversary, Vice-President Al Gore. The result was so close that a violent argument broke out in Florida, the state where his younger brother, Jeb, was Governor: a certain number of electors had not been able to vote, at least not in satisfactory conditions. The US Supreme Court, as the guarantor of respect for laws and institutions, intervened in the debate and decided in favour of the Republican candidate, halting the recount of votes that had been cast in that key state. This manipulation of destiny was in reality the work of conservative judges in the Supreme Court. Certain of them owed their careers to the Bush clan; others were closely linked to ultra-conservative Christian organizations. All of the latter had voiced their total support for the Governor of Texas, seeing in him, after years of struggle and frenzied activism, the means for them finally to win supreme power and impose their sectarian and retrograde views.

Eight months after the new head of the executive had assumed office, the magazine *Newsweek* published, in the same week as the attacks of 11 September, extracts from an unpublished book called *An Accidental President?* The question might have appeared provocative; it was in reality completely wrong. The victory of George W. Bush was anything but the result of an electoral accident. During this period, in the eyes of a large sector of American opinion, the verdict was that his administration appeared to be a disappointment: but few observers had gauged the profound transformation and the disquieting swing that had come about.

In American history, very many presidents had insisted on their religious roots, and strewn their speeches with references to the Bible, but never, before the arrival in the White House of George W. Bush, had religion weighed so extraordinarily heavily.

During his electoral campaign, the candidate had stated that Jesus was his favourite thinker 'because he saved my heart',[1] and in the course of his first address as President, he had declared that an 'angel rides the whirlwind and directs this storm', a strange and disconcerting allegory, close in tone to biblical prophecies.[2]

No sooner had he come to power than he decreed a National Day of Prayer for 20 January 2001, though one already existed, in May. Shortly afterwards, he announced a plan aimed at helping children experiencing learning difficulties in state schools to attend religious schools instead.

Hot on the heels of this, on 23 January 2001, he declared that he wished to suppress public financing for all family planning organizations, operating on American territory and abroad, that accepted every woman's right to have an abortion. This was a closely calculated and carefully timed decision. On the same day, thousands of extreme right-wing Christian militants, his electors, had gathered in Washington to demand the repeal of the law set out by the Supreme Court in 1973 legalizing abortion. 'To mix religion with politics in this way is unprecedented for a president who has been in power for only two weeks,' said Alan Lichtman, a historian at the American University of Washington.[3]

While delivering one of his first public speeches, George W. Bush was given an outright ovation when he claimed, 'The days of discriminating against religious institutions, simply because they are religious, must come to an end.'[4]

Shortly afterwards he vigorously defended one of the main demands of the ultra-conservative Christian (and even, in some cases, fundamentalist) organizations: that they should benefit handsomely from public funds to finance their welfare pro-grammes. This was a considerable source of increased wealth for these movements and their leaders, men of God but also shrewd company managers, most of them controlling vast personal fortunes. Ralph Mears calls it 'an administration that . . . is further to the right than either the first Bush or the Reagan administration. Across the board, it's obvious that the right wing is in control. And it's a right wing agenda that's being implemented.'[5]

During his campaign George W. Bush had stated that he incarnated a 'new type of Republican'. The reality turned out to be exactly the opposite.

The 'new alliance' that supported him resolutely turned its back on the Republican Party's traditional values and convictions, at least those defended by two of its historic leaders, Abraham Lincoln and Dwight D. Eisenhower. The Civil War had, after all, been a real ordeal for Lincoln. More than 140 years later, war was at the heart of the objectives of Christian fundamentalists, often racist and anti-semitic, yet extremely closely linked to Jewish neo-conservatives who supported Likud, the right-wing Israeli party in power in Jerusalem. For these groups the confrontation that they deemed necessary came on two levels.

On the level of domestic policies, it was a matter of successfully dismantling the entire welfare system, and support for minorities, that had been established over several decades, while imposing the most conservative religious values on the whole of American society. The Heritage Foundation, the bastion of this strategy, spoke of a second American revolution of 'cultural independence' whose aim was to undermine and destroy the existing multicultural society in the United States.

Abroad, their objective was to use the entirety of American power, especially its military force, to draw up a new geopolitical landscape in which Washington would be firmly in control. The first objective was to 'prevent any hostile power from dominating a region whose resources would, under consolidated control, be sufficient to generate global power', as the hawks in power around George W. Bush had written and publicly stated.[6]

'Jesus Seen as a Friend'

Shortly before leaving power, in a speech he gave in January 1961 that has remained famous, Eisenhower had referred to the existence of a 'military–industrial complex' which was posing a grave danger to American democracy. This combined omnipotence of the Pentagon and the arms industry was a source of anxiety for the former military chief.

The significance of this lobby and the threat it represented were frequently referred to during the following decades. But, to paraphrase Lenin, who judged shortly before his death in 1924 that 'multinational companies had taken over the planet', it was visibly true that this 'military–industrial complex' had reached its peak by taking over the Bush administration. In fact the men who devised and implemented defence policy, and who also drew up the new overall guidelines for American foreign policy, were indulging in what one observer called 'incestuous', but also fruitful, relations with the arms world and its main firms. I will set out the full details later.

The journalist Bob Woodward met the head of the American executive in August 2002 on his ranch in Crawford. He wrote this striking account.

> Bush says that on a day-to-day basis a president has to sort out a huge number of tactical battles on budgets and Congress resolutions, but he considers his work and his responsibilities as being much simpler. His father had regularly mocked the notion of 'vision' as being of no help. Thus I was all the more surprised to hear the young Bush saying, 'the job is . . . it's a vision thing'. This was another lesson I learnt. His vision includes an ambitious reorganization of the world through action (unilateral if necessary) to reduce suffering and bring about peace.[7]

The psychological portrait sketched by Woodward is interesting, but it still misses the essential thing.

Bush is not a serious reader. For long months, his sole bedside reading book was a biography of Sam Houston, one of the founders of Texas, a man he likes to identify with. And yet the first book that he had ever read from cover to cover, line by line, with close attention, radically changed his personality and the way he perceived the world. This book was the Bible – and he was almost 40 years old.

He had been married since 1977, and had joined the Methodist Church of which his wife Laura was a member. In the daytime he was a character without much of a personal history, who didn't stand out against his background and was considered by everyone as, in the words of someone close to him, 'merely his father's son'.[8] In the evenings he drank heavily. As the years went by his wife showed an increasing weariness and exasperation at this spineless behaviour. In 1985, at the age of 39, Bush, who by now had clocked up one professional failure after another, found himself in a deep crisis.

Howard Fineman relates in a report published by *Newsweek*, under the title 'Bush and God', how the future president managed to pull himself out of this morass with the help of one of his closest friends, Bob Evans, who is now his Secretary of Trade.

At the time, Evans too was going through serious personal and professional difficulties and he had joined a Bible study group. This programme, entitled 'Community Bible Study', laid out a timetable for the intensive study of one of the books of the New Testament for an entire year. A new chapter was tackled every week: it was reread in detail, and then discussed by a group of ten people. Evans had convinced George W. Bush to join him, and for two years the two friends immersed themselves deep in St Luke's Gospel, and had studied the conversion of Paul on the road to Damascus and the establishment of the Christian Church. According to Howard Fineman:

> Bush, who cares little for the abstract and a great deal for people, responded to the conversion story. He liked the idea of knowing Jesus as a friend. . . . The CBS program was a turning point for the future president in several ways. It gave him, for the first time, an intellectual focus. Here was the product of elite secular education – Andover, Yale and Harvard – who, for the first time, was reading a book line by line with rapt attention. And it was . . . the Bible. In that sense, Bush is a more unalloyed product of the Bible belt than his friends, who may have deeply studied something else in earlier days. A jogger and marathoner for years, Bush found in Bible study an equivalent mental and spiritual discipline, which he would soon need to steel himself for his main challenge in life to that point: to quit drinking. . . .

Bush says he never considered himself to be an alcoholic, and never attended an AA meeting. But it turned out he didn't have to. CBS was something akin to the same thing, part of what has since come to be called the 'small group' faith movement. It's a baby-boomerish mix of self-help, self-discipline, group therapy (without using what, for Bush, is a dreaded word) and worship. Whatever, it worked. As the world knows, Bush did quit drinking in the summer of 1986, after his and Evans's 40th birthday. 'It was "goodbye Jack Daniels, hello Jesus,"' said one friend from those days.[9]

During a short prayer breakfast, a few months after his election, Bush had confided: 'It [the faith] has sustained me in moments of success, and in moments of disappointment. Without it I would be a different person, and without it I doubt I'd be here today.'[10]

'New Birth'

'The President should be looking after matters of State and leaving those of the nation's soul in the hands of religious leaders', retorted Rob Boston, spokesman of an association devoted to the constitutional upholding of the separation between Church and State.[11] This response underlines the intensely serious and worrying problem confronting America today. For George W. Bush, as a *Newsweek* editorialist puts it, 'God is not neutral'. Religion imbues his thoughts, his actions, his vision of the world. Clear-cut ideas, a Manichean approach to problems – all resumed by this formula, uttered in the aftermath of 11 September: 'Those who are not with us, are against us'. After being 'born again' (a spiritual experience which many Americans – one citizen in four – also claims to have experienced) in 1986, Bush found, one year later, the framework that would permit him to combine his religious convictions with his political ambitions in an effective way. In 1987 he went to Washington and joined the team preparing his father's presidential campaign. He was entrusted – and this was obviously no coincidence – with relations with the various movements and organizations of the religious Right, in particular the Christian Coalition, created by Pat Robertson, a televangelist who delivers intransigent opinions in a smooth-toned voice, and whose personal fortune is estimated at 150 million dollars. 'His father wasn't comfortable dealing with religious types,' recalled Douglas Wead, one of his collaborators. But his son knew how to deal with them – they were on the same wavelength.[12] Throughout the campaign, George W. Bush went out of his way to try and insert the maximum number of biblical quotations into the electoral speeches delivered by his father – with mixed results.

When he decided, in 1993, to run for Governor of Texas, George W. Bush aroused the scepticism of his mother, who thought his younger brother Jeb was a better candidate for the same job in Florida. One year earlier his father had been beaten by Bill Clinton, and George W. had analysed at length the electoral reasons for this defeat, in the company of his 'political guru' Karl Rove, who is now part of his team in the White House.

The outgoing president had to a great extent failed because he had failed to win the votes of religious conservatives. Karl Rove has said publicly, 'you cannot alienate your base. You cannot alienate that 18% of religious conservatives. You don't mess with these people. They want you to be just as they are.'[13] This identification was obviously impossible in the case of Bush Sr, with his measured and distant tone, his manners of an East Coast patrician. Furthermore, in the eyes of extremist Christians, he had committed an unforgivable mistake: he had put pressure on Israel by forcing the then Prime Minister, Yitzhak Shamir, to sit down in 1991 at the negotiating table during the Madrid Conference. These Christian activists, in fact, espoused the most intransigent positions of the Israeli Right: a profoundly strange and ambiguous alliance, whose origin and motives I will be examining in more detail later.

Rove's formula 'You don't mess with these people. They want you to be just as they are' fitted George W. Bush like a glove. In 1993, as he was preparing to enter the lists for the post of Governor, he granted an interview to an Austin reporter, telling him that only believers in Jesus go to heaven.[14] This remark was theologically debatable and the journalist who reported it was Jewish. In the local and regional press, several journalists waxed indignant but Karl Rove was jubilant: his candidate's clumsy words constituted the most reliable key to winning the hearts and votes of the conservative Christian electorate, especially in the rural zones of the state of Texas. Throughout his campaign, Bush used pastors as intermediaries and electoral agents. They could be relied on to spread their net far and wide and supply accurate and up-to-the-minute polls on the state of mind of the future voters, their wishes and their pet hates.

Immediately after his victory he stated, 'I could not be governor if I did not believe in a divine plan that supersedes all human plans.'[15]

'You are Like Moses'

It's a really strange, highly personal faith, in the opinion of the journalists Lou Dubose and Molly Ivins, who have investigated the career of the current President in detail.[16] It is a fact that the certainty of being invested with a divine mission lies close to Bush's heart.

During his two first terms as Governor, combining his religious convictions with a judicious use of the media, he regularly appeared on the television programmes of several preachers. He was a great admirer of one of them, James Dobson, who ran an extreme right-wing religious group 'Focus on the Family', and also of James Robinson, a Texan televangelist from Fort Worth. When he was re-elected Governor in 1998, Bush invited Robinson to speak during the 'prayer breakfast' that marked the inauguration ceremony. In front of the future president, who listened with deep attention, Robinson recounted in detail to the company the long conversation he had had with God while driving along the highway between Arlington and Dallas.

At the beginning of 1999 George W. Bush started to toy with the idea of running for president. He first spoke about it to his mother Barbara, and shortly afterwards they both went to a church service. The sermon that day was about Moses's doubts as to his leadership qualities. Barbara confided to her son, 'You are like the figure of Moses.' Back home, they asked the advice of the pastor Billy Graham. Graham, a personal friend of the Bushes, was the most famous preacher in the United States, and the confidant

and spiritual adviser of several American presidents. The tapes on
which Richard Nixon illegally recorded all his conversations had
also revealed some rather edifying comments. In discussion with
the President in the Oval Office, Graham had notably referred to
'the domination of the Jews over the American media.'

Graham reassured Bush Jr at length about his capabilities. A
few weeks later, the Governor of Texas brought together in his
residence the principal pastors and leaders of the Christian Right.
'I am "called",' he told them, 'to seek higher office.'[17] Howard
Fineman describes the way he manoeuvred:

> Others tried to woo evangelicals by pledging strict allegiance on
> issues such as abortion and gay rights. 'Bush talked about his faith,'
> said Bauer, 'and people just believed him – and believed in him.'
> There was genius in this. The son of Bush One was widely, logi-
> cally, believed by secular voters to be a closet moderate. Suddenly,
> the father's burden was a gift: Bush Two could reach the base
> without threatening the rest. 'He was and is "one of us",' said
> Charles Colson, who sold the then Governor Bush on a faith-based
> prison program.[18]

Another decisive electoral phenomenon had probably not
escaped the notice of Bush or the sagacity of his adviser Karl
Rove: since 1985 the Southern states, profoundly conservative
and religious, had ceaselessly been tightening their grip on the
Republican Party.

David Frum, Bush's speechwriter in his first years as President,
relates a meeting in the Oval Office. Addressing the representatives of the main Protestant congregations, Bush confided to them,
'You know, I've had a problem with alcohol. Right now, I ought
to be in a bar in Texas instead of finding myself in the Oval Office.
There's only one reason why I'm in the Oval Office and not in a
bar: I found faith. I found God. I'm here because of the power of
prayer.'[19]

This was a confession which the writer Norman Mailer commented on with anxious irony. 'That is a dangerous remark. As
Kierkegaard was the first to suggest, we can never know for certain
to whom our prayers will go, nor from whom the answers will
come. Just when we think we are at our nearest to God, we could
be assisting the Devil.'[20]

These in turn are words which the Bush team is probably not ready either to hear or to accept. For David Frum, 'Bush comes from and speaks of a culture very different from that of the individualist Ronald Reagan. His culture is that of modern evangelism. To understand Bush's White House you need to understand the predominance of this belief.'[21] He reports the words that the American President addressed to him one morning as he was arriving at the White House to work with him: 'I haven't seen you at Bible study.'

A strange atmosphere predominates at the heart of the American executive: the wife of the Government Chief of Staff in the White House, Andrew Card, is a Methodist minister; the father of Condoleezza Rice, head of the National Security Council, is a preacher in Alabama; Michael Geerson, who directs the group that writes the President's speeches, is a graduate of Wheaton College in Illinois, nicknamed the 'evangelical Harvard'. This man subscribes to the prophecies of the extreme Christian Right, which believes in an imminent Armageddon, and the return of the Antichrist followed by the appearance of a new Messiah.

The entire staff of the White House takes part in daily Bible study groups. Nowadays, the Presidency resembles a huge prayer hall where, between two collective readings of the Old or New Testament, those in power govern the affairs of America and the whole world.

A 'Fatalist' Faith

After the events of 11 September, the religious tonality of the President's utterances became noticeably more intense. Bush had drawn the word 'evil' from his reading of the Psalms and used it extremely frequently in his speeches. For him, Osama bin Laden and his group were 'evil' incarnate. In November 2001, in an interview with *Newsweek*, he declared for the first time that Saddam Hussein was also 'evil' in person. 'The axis of evil', an expression used to describe Iraq, Iran and North Korea, was not a formula that sprang from nowhere. To characterize these three countries, David Frum had invented the term 'the axis of hatred'. His boss, Michael Geerson, 'tried to use the theological language

that Bush had been employing since 11 September', according to
Frum, and it was thus that, in his version, 'the axis of hatred'
became 'the axis of evil'.[22]

The historian Paul S. Boyer, Professor of History at the University of Wisconsin, has analysed the State of the Union address in
which the President declared, in particular, that Saddam Hussein
could unleash 'a day of horror like none we have ever known'.[23]
By expressing himself in these terms, according to Professor Boyer,
'he is not only playing upon our still-raw memories of 9/11. He
is also invoking a powerful and ancient apocalyptic vocabulary
that for millions of prophecy believers conveys a specific and
thrilling message of an approaching end – not just of Saddam, but
of human history as we know it.'[24] Bush likes to tell people that
his faith is 'simple'. Recently, an element of 'fatalism' has been
added to it, according to David Frum, who says, 'You have to do
your best and accept that everything is in God's hands. If you trust
in the fact that there is a God who rules the world, then you do
what's best and things work out.'[25]

These words confirm the analysis of Chip Bertlet, an expert on
ultra-conservative religious movements. 'Bush is very much into
the apocalyptic and messianic thinking of militant Christian evangelicals. He seems to buy into the worldview that there is a giant
struggle between good and evil culminating in a final confrontation. People with that kind of a worldview often take risks that
are inappropriate and scary because they see it as carrying out
God's will.'[26]

2

The 'Heritage' Connection

It all began in 1971. Protests against the Vietnam War were continuing to grow, and Richard Nixon seemed caught up in a direct confrontation with an entire sector of the American people. The final blow was the broadcast, in 1971, of the 'Pentagon Papers', containing a series of revelations on the underside of the war being waged in South East Asia. Compiled by a team under the Secretary of Defense, Robert McNamara, they underlined the grave disparities existing between the stated objectives and the real objectives. These papers had been leaked by a senior civil servant in the Pentagon, Daniel Ellsberg, and in spite of heavy pressure from the White House, a powerful daily newspaper, the *New York Times*, on receiving a favourable verdict from its legal advisers, decided to take the responsibility of publishing them. The impact was considerable. The dismay of the President reached its peak when he learnt that a copy of the voluminous dossier had found its way to the embassy of the USSR in Washington.

That same year, the National Chamber of Commerce had a memo circulated to the leaders of the business world and drawn up by Lewis Powell, a future judge in the Supreme Court. This text was to affect people's way of thinking profoundly: its impact was far-reaching.

In particular, Powell thought, 'the assault on the enterprise system is broadly based and consistently pursued. . . . The sources are varied and diffused. They include, not unexpectedly, the Communists, New Leftists and other revolutionaries who would destroy the entire system, both political and economic.' According to Powell, those who were leading the offensive were 'the college campus, the pulpit, the media, the intellectual and literary journals, the arts and sciences, and . . . politicians'.[1]

Powell's memo was not limited to this observation. It was also an analysis that took the offensive, and deeply impressed the conservatives in power, since it sketched out the strategy to be adopted not merely to reconquer the power and influence that had been lost, but also to establish an enduring domination over American politics and society. For him, the business world needed to combat and overcome this threat that came from the Left and the extreme Left, by dedicating all its know-how to active intervention. 'Strength lies in organization, in careful long-range planning and implementation, in consistency of action over an indefinite period of years, in the scale of financing available only through joint effort, and in the political power available only through united action and national organizations.'

A 'War Culture'

He also suggested that those organizations should use researchers, publish journals, write books, articles and polemics, and engage in a long-term effort to correct and counterbalance the profound bias emerging from university campuses. Finally, he advised that 'the national television networks should be monitored in the same way that textbooks should be kept under constant surveillance' and believed that this vigilance should also be applied to the judiciary system. Lewis Powell's comments constituted a veritable declaration of war on the counter-culture that occupied the front of the public and media stage, and on all moderate thoughts and ideas.

Men of immense wealth and ultra-conservative views were fascinated by these remarks. Imbued by the idea of a veritable 'war culture', they were ready to do battle with the America that they hated, 'eroded', in their eyes, 'by depravity and decadent ideas'. Thirty years later, during the presidency of George W. Bush, the same state of mind drives the extreme Right in America. Norman Mailer analyses it with trenchant lucidity:

That is a very large statement, but I can offer this much immediately: At the root of flag conservatism is not madness, but an undisclosed logic. While I am hardly in accord, it is, nonetheless, logical if you accept its premises. From a militant Christian point of view, America is close to rotten. The entertainment media are loose. Bare bellybuttons pop onto every TV screen, as open in their statement as wild animals' eyes. The kids are getting to the point where they can't read, but they sure can screw. So one perk for the White House, should America become an international military machine huge enough to conquer all commitments, is that American sexual freedom, all that gay, feminist, lesbian, transvestite hullabaloo, will be seen as too much of a luxury and will be put back into the closet again. Once we become a 21st century embodiment of the old Roman Empire, moral reform can stride right back into the picture with all the hypocrisy attendant on that. The military is obviously more puritanical than the entertainment media. Soldiers are, of course, crazier than any average man when in and out of combat, but the overhead command is a major everyday pressure on soldiers and could become a species of most powerful censor over civilian life.

To flag conservatives, war now looks to be the best possible solution. Jesus and Evel Knievel might be able to bond together, after all. Fight evil, fight it to the death! Use the word 15 times in every speech.[2]

At the start of the 1970s, these ultra-conservatives would probably already have been dreaming of an armed conflict capable of 'regenerating' America, if they had not had before their eyes the spectacle of Vietnam. This political and military failure plunged the country into one of the gravest moral crises in its history.

What they decided was this: they would bring the confrontation to their domestic scene, and would win over people's minds by influencing and manipulating their whole way of thinking. They acted with determination, method and perseverance. Christopher DeMuth, the president of the American Enterprise Institute, one of the principal conservative foundations, had stated, 'It takes at least 10 years for a radical new idea to emerge from obscurity.'[3]

This 'long march' was in reality to last thirty years. In 2001 the ultra-Right could henceforth savour the extent of its victory. Will Hutton expressed it clearly when he wrote, in The Observer:

The British and the other Europeans still don't understand. The United States has changed. Its political centre of gravity has moved away from the two liberal seaboards to the extraordinarily conservative South and Wild West, which want no truck with the outside world unless wholly on their terms. Since the Sixties, American conservatives have waged war on liberalism in any guise with an almost Leninist zeal and have now captured the American state. They intend to make victory pay.'[4]

In 1973 George Bush was Richard Nixon's ambassador to the United Nations, and nobody would have thought of predicting a great political future for him. He defended American policies in Vietnam to the Security Council, while at the same time his elder son George W. was finishing his period of military service in the Texas National Guard – the surest way to avoid being sent to fight in the mud and the paddy fields. Sometimes, at weekends, he would join his father in New York, in the suite of the Waldorf Astoria reserved all year long for the American envoy to the United Nations. He was most certainly unaware, and perhaps he never fully realized, that this was the year which marked the beginning of the ultra-conservative offensive whose absolute triumph would culminate three decades later with his election.

Billionaire and Recluse

For it was in 1973 that Richard Mellon Scaife entered the lists. This blond man with his piercing blue eyes and his reserved manners, aged 30 at the time, was over the years to earn the nickname of 'the financial father of the American Right'. He was the son of Sarah Mellon, the heir of the multimillionaire banker Andrew Mellon, considered during his lifetime, together with John D. Rockefeller, to be the richest man in the United States. When Richard Mellon Scaife's mother died in 1965, she left a personal fortune estimated at more than one billion dollars, and three richly endowed foundations, which her son would turn into so many tools for his activities.

Richard Scaife was a complex personality. Solitary, secretive, he was the owner of properties throughout the United States, but most often lived as a recluse in the huge family house in Pittsburgh where he had grown up, surrounded by an army of domestic servants.

He refused all interviews and any contact with the press, and many of those who had benefited from his generosity never met him. Pathologically timid, more interested in influence than in fame, he had had his name withdrawn from *Who's Who*, and his relationships with other people were fraught. 'He could', recounts one of his closest collaborators, 'behave like the most delightful and generous guy; but if he hated someone, not only would he sack him, he'd do everything in his power to make sure he never found a job in Pittsburgh again.'

Pat Minarcin, the former editor-in-chief of the magazine *Pittsburgher*, financed by Richard Scaife, relates the brief exchange he had had with the billionaire at the end of a working meeting. Pat Minarcin says, 'We were talking one time after a meeting and I said to him, "Is money power?" . . . He paused three or four seconds and looked at me really hard. He's just not used to people speaking to him on that level. He said, "I didn't use to think so, but the older I get the more I do." '5

Philanthropic action, tax-deductible, has always been one of the cornerstones of the American economic and financial world and its ability to influence political power. When he created his foundation, John D. Rockefeller, at that time the richest man in the world, had engaged the services of Frederick Gates, who was in charge of the American Baptist Education Society. The man of God would say repeatedly to the founder of Standard Oil: 'Your fortune is rolling up, rolling up like an avalanche! . . . You must keep up with it! You must distribute it faster than it grows! If you do not, it will crush you and your children and your children's children.'6

In the 1970s the two most richly endowed foundations in the United States, Ford and Rockefeller, were considered as liberal citadels of limited influence, since they 'distributed too little money to too many people', in the pertinent judgement of one conservative leader.

Richard Mellon Scaife, for his part, would adopt the opposite strategy. The heir to a fortune of billions, he is described by his ex-employee Pat Minarcin thus: 'He has the emotional maturity of a very angry 12-year-old, and he has all this money and he can do whatever he wants with it.'[7] He had always been interested in politics and in the most conservative causes.

In 1964 he had supported Barry Goldwater, who represented the right wing of the Republican Party, in his bid for the presidency. He financed his campaign and placed his private jet at his disposal. Goldwater's humiliating defeat at the hands of Lyndon Johnson completely took him aback. Later, even if he did give Richard Nixon a million dollars for his 1972 campaign, in the form of 344 different cheques so as to avoid tax as much as possible, he distanced himself from politicking.

'Winning the War of Ideas'

Scaife's strength, his principal psychological driving force, was that he in no way identified with the old conservative establishment. For him it was necessary to act, both by influencing and by intimidating – by means of new methods.

He had been captivated by Lewis Powell's text and in 1973 he launched the Heritage Foundation, created that year to become the weapon that would allow him, according to Scaife, to 'win the war of ideas'. He allocated 900,000 dollars to it.

Three years later, in 1976, he paid another 420,000 dollars into this organization – some 42 per cent of the foundation's total budget, estimated at the time to amount to 1 million dollars. This early support was 'absolutely critical' according to the president of the foundation, Edwin J. Feulner.[8]

Scaife had direct control over three foundations: the Sarah Scaife Foundation, whose assets were in 1997 evaluated at 302 million dollars, the Allegheny Foundation, with assets of 39 million dollars, and the Carthage Foundation, endowed with 24 million dollars. His two children, David and Jerry, were at the head of a fourth organization, the Scaife Family Foundation, whose assets amounted to 170 million dollars: it pursued the objectives assigned by their father. In thirty years, from 1967 to 1997,

Richard Scaife is said to have spent nearly 600 million dollars creating and maintaining many different institutes and ultra-conservative organizations, such as the Hoover Institution, at Stanford University, of which Condoleezza Rice was a Fellow; the American Enterprise Institute, two of whose pillars are now the hawk Richard Perle and Lynn Cheney, the wife of the Vice-President; and the Cato Institute and a myriad of other foundations acting in the social and juridical realms, and even in the world of education.

But over the years, the jewel in Scaife's crown remained the Heritage Foundation, which, in the terms of one of its vice-presidents, Burton Yale Pines, was the base for the 'storm troops of the conservative revolution' – men with an ideological vision of American society. For the directors of Heritage, any progressive measure, from Franklin Roosevelt's New Deal onwards, constituted 'an assault on founding principles articulated in the 18th century'.[9]

Over the years, more than half of its budget was devoted to the marketing of ideas. Its collaborators, who actively intervened in the world and reacted to the latest developments, wrote articles and studies covering every field of American politics: the Communist threat, the reduction of welfare, the boosting of the military budget, the central place of religion, or the struggle against the trade unions.

Each and any member of Congress, on the eve of a debate or a vote on an important law, might find on his or her desk a report from Heritage analysing the bill to be presented, and proposing solutions. The Heritage Foundation provided the Senate and the House of Representatives, as well as the media and the public, with these studies. It had invented, in the words of one observer, 'the attaché case memo'.

For Walter Mears, the vice-president of Associated Press, the conservative movement is 'a growth industry'. He says of Heritage, 'given the shift in political life on the Hill, they've been in the right place at the right time'.[10] This is confirmed by Thomas Bray, the director of the *Detroit News*, who says, 'The brilliant thing they did was to figure out how to get their viewpoint on your desk the next morning. Every day you open up the mail and there's a blizzard of releases from Heritage. It may not be the most thorough, or in depth, but it's there and it spells out a definite viewpoint and suggests ways of looking at things that might not have occurred to you.'[11] For one observer of public life,

> Modern Washington resembles an immense film set in which nothing is left to chance: each appearance, each declaration is carefully conceived to cause the maximum political effect. The genius of Heritage has been to apprehend this reality of life in the American capital and to use its financial means to impose its views. By deliberately overestimating its importance, Heritage is basically like a cinema company and it has become a key actor by putting on a daily show. It's the Walt Disney of Washington and the impact of its messages, whether it's a question of the privatization of social security or flat-rate taxation, can only increase.

From the point of view of Richard Scaife, if it was necessary to dethrone the liberal establishment in power in the federal capital, it was also going to be necessary to change the tone and tendency of the media. Immured in his solitude, he lived with the obsession and the certainty that the American Republic was threatened by mortal danger. Many various plots were endeavouring to undermine it. He had confided that one of his heroes was John Edgar Hoover, the director, until his death in 1972 of the FBI, who, in the words of one humorist, 'had always suspected Senator McCarthy of basically being a Communist agent'. Curiously enough for a man who believed in the power of ideas, Richard Mellon Scaife read little. One book, however, had influenced him a great deal: *The Spike*, written by the journalist Arnaud De Borchgrave, who was to become one of his friends and the editor of the conservative daily the *Washington Times*, financed by the Moonies. The *Times* would give its unstinting support to Reagan and the Bush family. *The Spike* tells the story of a young journalist who finds himself being manipulated as a pawn in the magisterial plot set up by the Soviet Union to control the world.

The Four Sisters

Scaife, though heir to a vast fortune, had not been the sole financier to help bring the Heritage Foundation into being. William Coors, the beer magnate, had in 1973 given 250,000 dollars. The Coors group, set up in 1877 by Adolphe Coors in Colorado, continued to be a family business, long famous for its anti-trade-union, anti-homosexual, anti-minority positions, and its policy of discrimination against women. In 1978 the Coors family had engaged in a show of strength with the unions, employing hundreds of non-union workers, who, together with the non-strikers who joined them, all voted for the suppression of the existing union.

In 1984 William Coors spoke in Denver, Colorado, in front of an assembly of businessmen and businesswomen representing several minorities, including a great number of black Americans. His comments petrified the gathering. He said, 'one of the best things they [slave traders] did for you is to drag your ancestors over here in chains'. He went on to claim that the weakness of the Zimbabwean economy was due to the 'lack of intellectual capacity' of black Africans.[12] Faced with the outrage that greeted his remarks, Coors pretended that his words had been taken out of context and threatened the newspaper that had reported them, the *Rocky Mountain News*, with legal action.

In order to counter this negative publicity and the threats of a boycott issuing from Hispanic and Afro-American groups, his group paid millions of dollars to organizations representing these minorities.

But this attitude was a smokescreen that failed to hide the essential. The Coors Foundation kept up extremely close relations with ultra-conservative organizations, in particular the principal figures on the Christian Right. The leader of the Moral Majority, pastor Jerry Falwell, benefited from the largesse of Coors, as did Pat Robertson, the head of the Christian Coalition, two men who are today very close to George W. Bush. Coors also supports Bob Simond of the 'National Association of Christian Educators/ Citizens for Excellence in Education', which claims to be 'putting born-again Christians on every school board in America'.[13] He also helped the Free Congress Foundation, known for its far-right positions.

Curiously enough, during recent years it has been possible to observe a growing split between the Coors firm and his foundation. The latter continues to be an important source of financing for the extreme Right, whereas the company leadership has adopted a socially and financially 'progressive' attitude towards its gay and lesbian employees. But as one analyst commented, 'this change may be due more to the desire to win new sectors of the beer market than to a real development in the way people think'.

Two other important foundations complete this array of ultra-conservative forces.

The Olin Foundation, based in New York, draws its revenue from a family business which has made a fortune from the manu-facture of munitions and chemical products. It has, of course, financed Heritage, American Enterprise, and the Hoover Institu-tion. The foundation also subsidized conservative academics such as Allan Bloom, who received 3.6 million dollars to direct, at Chicago University, the John M. Olin center for research on the theory and practice of democracy.

Bloom, known throughout the world for an essay that described the effects of the 1960s and the decline of the American acade-mic world, was also the professor and intellectual guru of Paul Wolfowitz, the current Deputy Secretary of Defense, the veri-table theorist of the hawks now in power in Washington. Irving Kristol, a former Trotskyist militant who later became a fierce anti-Communist and one of the leaders of the conservative Right during the Reagan administration, has also benefited from Olin's largesse. He received more than 380,000 dollars between 1992 and 1994 as the Olin researcher at the American Enterprise Insti-tute. His son, William Kristol, is at present considered to be one of the most influential thinkers in the current American adminis-tration. He is also the editor of the neo-conservative magazine *Weekly Standard*, which is entirely financed by the press magnate Rupert Murdoch, who is close to the Bush family.

William Simon, the president of the Olin Foundation, and a former finance minister under Richard Nixon, has detailed his efforts to convince the business world to stop subsidizing univer-sity programmes that have a 'left-wing' tendency. For Simon, 'Cor-porations have this habit of supporting their own demise. I used to make a habit of asking corporate officers and trustees why they were giving money to the very people who seek to destroy capi-talism and free markets in this country.'[14]

The last of these 'four sisters' of conservative philanthropy is the Lynde and Harry Bradley Foundation, whose assets exceed 420,000 million dollars.

Lynde and Harry Bradley made their fortune manufacturing radio and electronic components. Harry's extreme right-wing positions have led him to become an active member and a financier of the John Birch Society, an extreme right-wing anti-Communist, homophobic and sexist organization that defends white supremacism. Robert Welsh, who founded this movement in 1958, regularly took part as an 'invited speaker' at the gatherings of the firm's sales forces. The Coors Foundation too has financed the John Birch Society.

Harry Bradley was also a supporter of Fred Schwartz, the founder of the Christian anti-Communist crusade. The Allen Bradley Company, one of the biggest employers in the city of Milwaukee, was one of the last to accept racial integration, and only when faced with the combined effect of public and juridical pressure. In 1968, out of 7,000 employees, the company had only 32 blacks and 14 Latinos.

The financial power of the foundation was multiplied tenfold in 1985 when Allen Bradley was bought up by one of the main arms-manufacturing firms, Rockwell International Corporation, a conglomerate working for the defence sector and the air force.

The Bradley Foundation subsidizes, in particular, National Empowerment Television (NET), the most powerful communications weapon in the hands of the extreme Right. Coordinated and directed by Paul Weyrich, one of the founders of Heritage and the Free Congress Foundation, NET can be received in millions of homes with cable, and propagates a whole extremist Christian ideology. NET supplies air-time to tens of extreme right-wing organizations such as the Christian Coalition or the National Rifle Association, which supports the continuing free sale of firearms.

'The Voice of Wisdom and Common Sense'

Over the years, the 'messages' of the extreme Right, transmitted through the organizations created, were carefully orchestrated and amplified into a mass movement. Techniques of marketing, political relations and management were employed to hammer out these messages until they became, in the eyes of the majority of public opinion, the 'voice of wisdom and common sense'. 'The welfare system doesn't work any more' or 'state schools have failed': these were all messages that were dinned into the minds of the public via many different channels. Detailed case studies, and concrete individual examples were used to back up these demonstrations.

This orchestration was based on the 'Mighty Wurlitzer' technique, an enigmatic formulation used by the CIA to describe propaganda that is tirelessly repeated and re-echoed through numerous channels until public opinion considers what it hears to be the truth.

According to a study published by the organization 'People for the American Way', 'right-wing foundations have developed a truly comprehensive funding strategy, providing grants to a broad range of groups, each promoting right-wing positions to their specific audiences'.[15] A considerable number of political conceptions or ideas which had long been discredited or swept aside as being out of synch with the dominant tendency were thus set back at the heart of the debates.

The coming to power of Ronald Reagan, in 1980, constituted the first great victory of the ultra-conservative movement – and of Heritage. The foundation supplied the new administration with people and ideas. It had drawn up, in the same year as the election, a 'mandate for leadership', in the form of 3,000 pages divided into twenty volumes. Reagan's entire future programme, subsequently described as a 'conservative revolution', was contained and developed in these texts. They tackled the 'Star Wars' project as well as massive reductions in welfare. A 1,093-page summary was produced for Reagan's transition team.[16] This text, according to one of its writers, had really become the new Bible for the new administration – they drew their ideas from it, and 'a clear vision of the aims to be achieved and the methods to succeed in doing so'.

Edwin J. Feulner, the president of Heritage, had, a few years earlier, summarized the strategy adopted: 'We don't just stress credibility

. . . We stress an efficient, effective delivery system. Production is one side; marketing is equally important.' To which we can add the remarks of David Mason, one of the vice-presidents of the foundation: 'we come up with the ideas and then provide the research and analysis to people who will champion those ideas in the political arena'.[17] As *The Economist* wrote twenty years later:

> The right's real advantage lies in commitment and organisation. Many of the conservative think-tankers grew-up in the 1960's and 1970's, when conventional wisdom held that government spending would solve most problems. They recruited a small army of passionate maverick dissenters, notably academics who felt marginalised at those left-leaning universities. Even now, when they are rich and powerful, there is something endearingly rabid and unhygienic about many think-tankers.[18]

3

The War of Ideas

In December 2000, just after his contested election, George W. Bush received a memo from David Horowitz advising him to 'assign greater weight to intellectual capital and moral credibility than to management skills . . . the close vote and contested election sharply increases the value of appointees able to finesse the "no mandate" pressures that will be placed on the governor.'[1]

The words of Horowitz, the President's unofficial adviser, were noted. His trajectory illustrates, in a fascinating and exaggerated way, the broken commitments of the 1960s, the support for the most conservative ideas, the links with the philanthropic patrons of the extreme Right such as Mellon Scaife or the Bradley Foundation. It reveals a bellicose state of mind, as found in those ideologists driven by a veritable civil war logic to combat the progressive, liberal America that they consider to be an adversary beyond redemption.

Noam Chomsky, the old figurehead of American leftism, a respected linguist but a controversial thinker, declared of Horowitz, who was increasing his attacks on him, 'I haven't read Horowitz. I didn't use to read him when he was a Stalinist and I don't read him today. Haven't seen it.'[2]

In 1959, at the age of 20, Horowitz, standing on the steps of the University of California, Berkeley, took up the cudgels in defence of a young conscientious objector who was demonstrating against the war and military lobbies. In 1962 he was a leading light in the student movement involved in violent demonstrations against the police, and published his first book, *Student*, which sold 25,000 copies. *Student*, a diatribe against the conformism and boredom of the 1950s, began with a line taken from the cinema director Ingmar Bergman, 'I've only ever prayed a single prayer in my life: use me.'

The same year, he went with his family to London where he stayed for six years. David Horowitz became very close to the Bertrand Russell Peace Foundation, considered by specialists to be entirely the tool of Soviet propaganda, and also to Isaac Deutscher, the author of a monumental biography of Trotsky. At that time, Horowitz's writings – and there were many of them – were aimed at 'the reconstruction of socialist theory after Stalin'.[3]

'The Disenchantment of a Radical'

In 1968, just back from a California where the student movement was in a state of ferment, he became editor of the magazine *Ramparts*, which became one of the emblematic publications of the New Left. In 1974 David Horowitz acted as Jean Genet's guide, when the latter came to San Francisco to support the cause of the Black Panthers. In Oakland, on the other side of the San Francisco Bay, they met the movement's leader, Huey Newton, who had just returned from China. The visit led to an impassioned exchange between Newton and Horowitz on the revolutionary virtues of Maoism. China, at the time, was embroiled in the bloody Cultural Revolution.

When Horowitz left, he was completely enthralled by the black leader, and had no inkling of the fact that he was a dangerous and unbalanced man. He abused cocaine and, in July 1974, assassinated a young prostitute before fleeing to Cuba, where Fidel Castro was delighted to offer him political asylum. For Horowitz this came as a profound shock, followed, five months later, by a new drama. Newton's successor as the head of the Black Panthers asked him to recommend a person capable of reorganizing and controlling the movement's finances. His choice fell on a woman who had collaborated on *Ramparts*, 42-year-old Betty van Patter. On 13 December 1974 her body was discovered in San Francisco Bay, with a massive head wound.

'The van Patter case', said one observer, 'was to haunt the Bay for two decades.'[4] The murder was never cleared up but, according to the investigators, Betty van Patter probably discovered that the Black Panthers were involved in drug trafficking, racketeering and prostitution; once she had become a potentially troublesome witness, they eliminated her.

This death plunged Horowitz into a 'clinical depression. For an entire year, I woke every morning in tears.'[5] The drama probably led to a psychological trauma. Little by little, Horowitz distanced himself from the leftist movement of which he had been one of the leaders. In 1979 he published in *The Nation* a long article entitled 'A Radical's Disenchantment', in which he criticized his companions for their moral indifference to the repression and genocide then happening in Vietnam and in the Cambodia of the Khmer Rouge.[6]

The final break came about when in 1984 he called for Ronald Reagan to be re-elected. Two years later, speaking at the University of California, Berkeley, where he had made his political debut, he harangued his audience with the words: 'You are in fact in league with the darkest and most reactionary forces of the modern world, whose legacies – as the record attests – are atrocities and oppression on a scale unknown in the human past.'[7]

In 1988 he wrote the speeches of Bob Dole, George Bush's rival during the Republican primaries. The following year, he published a new book, *Reflections on the Sixties*. Then he set up the Center for Popular Culture: all the good fairies of the extreme Right came to gather round its cradle and give it their blessing. In its first year Richard Mellon Scaife gave it 25,000 dollars, the Olin Foundation 20,000 dollars and the Bradley Foundation 40,000 dollars. These contributions were to rise continuously over the following years, finally representing two-thirds of its annual budget. At the beginning of 2000 Horowitz's institution had received more than 9 million dollars; 4.1 million came from Richard Mellon Scaife, 3.6 million from Bradley and 1.4 million from Olin. At the same time as he was being financed by the Christian extreme Right, Horowitz had for many years enjoyed close links with the Jewish neo-conservatives currently in power in Washington.

On his website Horowitz attacks all those whom he suspects of belonging to a 'fifth column', whether they be a university professor opposed to the war, or a member of Congress who is uneasy with George W. Bush's policies. In reply to one reader, he declared, 'Thirty Muslim states, thirty states without a democracy. Until the Muslim world gets past theocracy and learns tolerance, the Jews need to be armed to the teeth and much more ruthless with their enemies than they have been, since when it comes to the Jews fear is the only kind of respect the Arab world will give them.'[8]

His link with the hawks dates to the end of the year 1987. Elliott Abrams, then US Assistant Secretary of State for Inter-American Affairs, suggested that he go to Nicaragua to fight the Sandinista regime. Horowitz stayed for nearly a year in Managua, dispensing his opinions in the restaurant of the Hotel Intercontinental to trade unions, journalists and political opponents desirous of combating the current pro-Cuban and pro-Soviet regime. Abrams would be removed from the political scene shortly afterwards for his central role in the Iran–Contra scandal (the illicit financing of the anti-Sandinista rebels by the American administration, in part with Saudi Arabian money).

When he came to draw up his administration in 1988, Bush Sr had left him on the sidelines. Bush Jr, on the other hand, put him in charge of Middle Eastern affairs at the National Security Council in the White House. This was a key post for this partisan of a hard line towards the Arab world who supported an intransigent attitude towards the Palestinians on the part of the Israeli government. Abrams was very close to Richard Perle and Paul Wolfowitz. Horowitz, alongside them, is one of the thinkers of this ultra-conservative administration.

Thinking about his own itinerary, the historian Isaac Deutscher, a former Communist, declares that we need to 'continue to see the world in white and black, but now the colours are differently distributed'.[9] These remarks from Horowitz's intellectual guru are applicable, word for word, to his disciple.

To pillory and defame your adversaries – or those you consider to be such – is one of the main tactics of these conservative extremists. Michael Joyce, the president of the Bradley Foundation, congratulates himself on the activism of Horowitz: 'He's an extremely articulate man and a very determined fighter. I think he brings a great deal of intellectual power and energy to his work.'[10] And sometimes he oversteps the mark. In 1996, he attacked the journalist Steve Wasserman who had just been signed on by the *Los Angeles Times*. In an interview with the magazine *Buzz*, he accused him of having belonged to an urban guerrilla group created at Berkeley and nicknamed 'the red family'. In a long letter, Wasserman refuted these allegations and Horowitz seemed to back-pedal. However, shortly afterwards, in the periodical *Salon*, he resumed his attacks, writing of the leftist splinter-group that they 'hoped to launch a "war of liberation" in America, and Wasserman was one of their foot soldiers'.[11]

In 1992 the journalist David Brock published a long article questioning the credibility of Anita Hill. This young black woman was accusing her superior, the conservative judge Clarence Thomas, who had been marked down for a future seat on the Supreme Court, of sexual harassment. The president of the Olin Foundation, William Simon, was at the time the president of the citizens' committee supporting the candidacy of Justice Thomas.

The article published in the conservative magazine *American Spectator*, completely financed by Richard Mellon Scaife, and the Olin and Bradley Foundations, notably described Anita Hill as 'a little bit nutty and a little bit slutty'.[12] Those in charge of the Bradley Foundation paid Brock to write a book about it all: it was published under the title *The Real Anita Hill*. All the ultra-conservative networks mobilized to ensure it made a splash. The extreme right-wing Christian presenter Russ Limbaugh read out extracts from the book on his radio programme that had an audience of over 2 million listeners; the *Wall Street Journal* devoted a page-long editorial to it, and the literary supplement of the *New York Times* gave it a serious and respectful treatment. The book became a best-seller, and the author David Brock, who has since distanced himself from those ultra-conservative circles, believes now that the accusations brought by Anita Hill were well founded.

The Arkansas Project

Brock has depicted Mellon Scaife and the other main treasurers of the conservative offensive as a handful of wealthy fanatics.[13]

As soon as he was elected President in November 1992, Bill Clinton became Scaife's obsession. In his eyes, Clinton incarnated all the amorality and the anti-war leftism of the 1960s. Later, Scaife also described the President as a 'sexual predator'. He would buy all the magazines, including the most sordid tabloids, accusing Clinton of being mixed up with drugs, or having illegitimate children. The mysterious death of Vince Foster, a White House adviser and a former partner of Hillary Clinton in her legal practice, rekindled his obsession with a plot. Indeed, he later confided to John Kennedy Jr, editor of the magazine *George*: 'Listen, he [Bill Clinton] can order people done away with at his will. He's got the entire federal government behind him. . . . God, there must be 60 people out there who had died mysteriously.'[14]

It was all completely off-the-wall stuff, as was the 'Arkansas Project' that he financed in full.

It all started towards the end of 1993, during an onboard fishing expedition. Richard Scaife was accompanied by David Henderson, a conservative activist and public relations adviser, Steven Boynton, a Washington lawyer and his right-hand man Richard Larry. This former Marine, 63 years old, with cut-and-dried ideological views, had been working for Scaife for thirty years. He hated Clinton, to such an extent that one of his associates recalls, 'at the mention of Clinton he became almost hyperthyroid'.[15] Just like his boss, who could be heard openly expressing his determination to throw that guy out of the White House!

Henderson and Boynton claimed to have contacts in Arkansas, the state where Clinton had been Governor, that would enable them to reveal the extent of the scandals surrounding the President. In particular, Henderson had met David Hale, a minor lawyer from Little Rock, who became one of the prosecution witnesses against Bill Clinton in the Whitewater affair, a real-estate programme that had gone sour. Hale, accused of fraud by the Small Business Association, was in fact an important asset in the long inquiry into the President's dealings that was led by the ultra-conservative Special Prosecutor, Kenneth Starr – another man who greatly benefited from Mellon Scaife's financial generosity: the billionaire had Starr appointed to the conservative university of

Pepperdine, near Los Angeles, an establishment of which he is the patron.

In his written replies to the *Washington Post* which had asked him for an interview, the billionaire had explained that his support for the project stemmed from his doubts as to 'the desire of the *Washington Post* and other major newspapers to carry out a full inquiry into the disturbing scandals emerging from Clinton's White House'. And he added, 'I'm not the only one to have the feeling that the press shows a leaning to a Democrat administration. That's why I provided money to independent journalists investigating these scandals.'

The demand for rigour so publicly expressed by Mellon Scaife hardly corresponded to reality. The newspaper chosen to publish these future 'revelations', *American Spectator*, was an ultra-conservative magazine with a circulation of 30,000. Scaife had injected over 3.3 million dollars into it. The independent journalist was none other than David Brock, the man who had written the polemic on Anita Hill. As for the investigators, they boiled down to a former member of the Mississipi police, now turned private detective, Rex Armistead.

The first article to appear reported the words of members of the Arkansas police stating that they would escort Governor Clinton on secret romantic assignations. The report mentioned a woman 'called Paula'. This, of course, was Paula Jones. Richard Scaife spent a total of 2.4 million dollars in his attempt to discredit Clinton. But there were some shocking implications to the whole affair. The investigator Rex Armistead, who received over 353,517 dollars, several times met Hickman chief deputy to Prosecutor Kenneth Starr. Ewing, an ultra-conservative Christian, born again like George W. Bush, had turned Clinton's fall into a personal crusade – just as his boss had.

Paula Jones, now surrounded by a team of excellent lawyers, had been able to launch her famous suit accusing Clinton of sexual harassment thanks to money from Scaife's circuits. And Starr's other witness for the prosecution, David Hale, stated that he too had benefited from the billionaire's generosity.

As for any proofs against the President, they were nonexistent, and the scenarios that had been dreamt up were quite fantastic.

The investigator Armistead asserted that not only did Clinton use cocaine while he was Governor, but that he was covering for a major drugs network based in Latin America and operating through Mena, the main airport in Arkansas. Richard Scaife was so dissatisfied with these results that in 1997 he abruptly informed the editor of *American Spectator* that from now on he would no longer give the magazine his financial support.

However, Clinton and what he represented – a generation of baby-boomers, originally somewhat anti-establishment but now moderate in its reformism – continued to stoke the hatred of the conservatives. Another illustration of this can be found in the behaviour of Timothy Flanigan. It had all happened in 1992, when Bush Sr was fighting for re-election. His entourage, of which Flanigan was part, was trying to discredit his Democrat rival. Flanigan obtained Clinton's passport dating from his days as an Oxford student, in an attempt to discover traces of a trip to Moscow, which would enable him to insinuate that the future President had perhaps been brainwashed or manipulated by the KGB.

Today, Flanigan is an associate legal adviser at the White House, one of President Bush's assistants. He regards Kenneth Starr as a moderate, and this father of fourteen children is, of course, a fierce opponent of abortion. The Federalist Society of which he is a member has given him 700,000 dollars to write a biography of a former President of the Supreme Court.

The current energy minister, Spencer Abraham, was one of the people who set up this ultra-conservative society, active in the legal field. Another of the eminent members is the Solicitor General, Theodore B. Olson, who represented Kenneth Starr, and advised Paula Jones and Monica Lewinsky. He is close to Richard Scaife, who finances this organization too: we owe him this memorable observation: 'It's easy to imagine an infinite number of situations where the government might legitimately give out false information.'[16]

'A Vast Right-Wing Conspiracy'

The lawyer Hillary Clinton expressly named Richard Scaife as the principal figure in 'a vast rightwing conspiracy that has been conspiring against my husband since the day he announced for president'.[17] James Carville, Clinton's electoral adviser, described the Pittsburgh billionaire as 'the archconservative godfather in [a] heavily funded war against the president'.[18]

The network of jurists, members of the Federalist Society, whether judges, prosecutors or lawyers, was over the eight years of Clinton's Presidency to wage an incessant guerrilla war against the decisions taken by the government, bringing more and more legal actions across the country, and putting a brake on the application of federal measures.

To bend the law and the juridical framework in a much more conservative, restrictive and repressive direction is their objective. They want, among other things, to eliminate the welfare system, bilingual facilities in education, positive discrimination (which lays down quotas for minorities) and even the right to take the government to court.

Between 1994 and 1996 Scaife paid out 525,000 dollars to the Federalist Society, via two of his foundations.[19]

Two other conservative juridical organizations were also to benefit from Scaife's generosity. Landmark Legal Foundation received, in 1973, 375,000 dollars, and Judicial Watch almost 500,000 dollars. The latter was to lodge eighteen complaints against the Clinton administration, while Landmark took pains to block the initiatives of the Department of Justice, in particular its inclination to launch an inquiry into the somewhat unorthodox methods used by Special Prosecutor Starr against Bill Clinton.

The vigilance and the implacable demand for rigour insisted on by these jurists were not much in evidence at the time of the contested election of George W. Bush in November 2000. While the counting of the votes in the state of Florida aroused an intense polemic, the Federal Supreme Court, on 12 December, halted a new recount and annulled a decree of the Florida Supreme Court. This intervention made the Republican candidate the winner.

Two of the conservative judges who thus swung the scales in George W. Bush's favour were active members of the Federalist Society. One was Justice Scalia, whose son, by pure coincidence, was to be given an important post in the new administration; the other was Clarence Thomas, the man who had been accused of sexual harassment by Anita Hill and saved by a press campaign orchestrated by the ultra-conservatives. It was also discovered that Justice Thomas's wife worked for the Heritage Foundation and that she participated in a working group preparing future nominations in the Bush administration; she declared that she saw no conflict of interests between her activity and the crucial role played by her husband during the presidential election.

The Left has Lost the War of Ideas

This decisive boost to the Republican candidate and the extent of the attacks being made on Bill Clinton could not, however, conceal an underlying reality: in 2000 the American Left had totally lost the war of ideas.

> Take a tour of our nation's cultural landscape as the century turns, and you find that ideas once considered ideologically revanchist are in full bloom, funded by right-wing donors. While many of the most promising intellectual talents on the left have eschewed the 'real' world of public discourse for the cloistered confines of narrow academic concerns, the right has been taking its message to 'the people' in the form of bestselling book after bestselling book. Authors like the late Allan Bloom, Jude Wanniski, Charles Murray, Marvin Olasky, Bill Bennett, Dinesh D'Souza, Francis Fukuyama and Samuel Huntington, to pick just a few, have all written books in the past two decades that have transformed our political and cultural discourse on issues that are central to the way we organize ourselves as a society. Yes, they had the advantage of a powerful echo chamber within the punditocracy and the world of conservative opinion media. Yes, many of the books played into a few prejudices that many Americans may have already held but did not consider respectable to utter in polite company. But most important, these people wrote books directed at a mass audience and received funding and support from conservative sources that understood the fundamental importance of the battle of ideas.[20]

The Bradley Foundation, at the end of 1999, could list over 400 books that it had financed over the last fourteen years. Michael Joyce said, 'We have the conviction that most of the other media are derivative from books. Books are the way that authors put forth more substantial, more coherent arguments. It follows that if you want to have an influence on the world of ideas, books are where you want to put your money.'[21]

This vast ultra-conservative offensive designed at overturning the social system and the convictions of a majority of Americans reached a turning point with the publication in 1984 of *Losing Ground: American Social Policy 1950–1980*. The author, Charles Murray, constituted a veritable textbook case in terms of manipulation and marketing: the media and the public were to have an unknown figure imposed on them as one of the most important contemporary thinkers, whose pseudo-scientific theories aimed at making racism respectable.

Murray was living, quite unknown, in Iowa, and his intellectual production was limited to a few polemics which were mostly never published. He sent one of them to the conservative magazine *National Interest* whose editor was Irving Kristol, the guru of the neo-conservatives. Delighted by what he read, Kristol suggested that Murray turn it into a book, and immediately found him financial support and a working environment with the Olin Foundation and the Manhattan Institute, another conservative body. The latter orchestrated an astonishing campaign to sell Murray to the public: 700 copies of the book were sent, before publication, to journalists, politicians and academics. Public relations experts were given the task of transforming a nobody into a celebrity. Journalists were paid between 500 and 1,500 dollars each to take part in a seminar at which Murray presented his ideas.

This manifesto of the extreme Right defended the idea that poverty was not the result of economic crises, marked by lay-offs and business closures, or even of racial or sexual discrimination, but was, first and foremost, the consequence of personal failures. Murray stated that most government programmes designed to tackle poverty were misconceived and should be suppressed. He called in particular for the end of welfare programmes for single mothers, as well as 'support for families with dependent children', housing benefit and food coupons.

'We tried to provide more for the poor,' said Charles Murray, 'and we created more poor instead.'[22]

His words came at just the right moment. In 1984, the Reagan administration was leading a hard-hitting offensive to dismantle all those welfare programmes which constituted, in the conservatives' eyes, a culture which inevitably encouraged poverty.

If his book became a reference work, a bedside tome and a bestseller, this was also because its publication coincided with a period when a broad sector of American opinion was questioning what it had taken for granted about the validity of programmes of government aid, especially those in favour of the most disadvantaged. As a Washington observer commented, at this time, the 'religious and confessional creed of the Reagan administration with regard to the weakest could be summarized in the formula "Heaven helps those who help themselves" '.[23]

Losing Ground had opened a breach that its author would endeavour to widen a few years later when in 1994 he published *The Bell Curve* with the psychologist Richard Hernstein, of Harvard University. The book's subtitle ran: 'Intelligence and Class Structure in American Life'.

From 1986 to 1991 the Bradley Foundation paid Charles Murray a salary of 90,000 dollars a year, a sum which had been increased to 113,000 dollars in 1991.[24] The author was also a researcher at the Manhattan Institute, a conservative think tank, one of whose founders had been William Casey, the director of the CIA under Ronald Reagan.

So Murray was at the heart of an ultra-conservative machinery which conceived his works as so many missiles launched against the federal state and the liberal establishment. *The Bell Curve* highlighted and developed certain arguments from the previous book, adding the genetic theories of its co-author Hernstein. According to an article in the *New York Times*, Hernstein predicted that the more meritocratic a society became, the more individuals with a low IQ would sink to the bottom of the economic ladder. They would intermarry and produce offspring of low intelligence.[25]

One of the book's central theses claimed that intelligence stemmed from race. For the authors, poverty was not the result of socio-economic or political conditions, but of inferior genetic characteristics.

Murray and Hernstein proposed sweeping reforms so as simultaneously to eradicate poverty and the threat of an increasingly numerous 'sub-class' by eliminating all welfare programmes, and replacing them with coercive measures designed to modify people's behaviour. It was not a question of making the poor classes able to find work and independence, but of regulating their behaviour, since the authors considered them incapable of controlling and directing their own lives.

The publication of this work aroused numerous controversies. Experts pointed out the lacunas, contradictions and misleading arguments that ran through the book's thesis.

The Manhattan Institute, which had successfully launched Murray's previous book and employed him as a researcher, distanced itself from the whole business when faced with the extent of the polemics and dissociated itself from him. But his other sponsors did not have the same scruples. The Bradley Foundation increased the sum it allocated him annually to 163,000 dollars, after the publication of *The Bell Curve*, and the American Enterprise Institute of Washington suggested taking him on as a consultant and researcher. This organization, created in 1943 to combat the progressive policies of the New Deal launched by Franklin Roosevelt, had gone on to become a staging post for the business world before unavoidable ultra-conservative philanthropists such as Richard Scaife helped it to develop even further.

The Bell Curve, a *succès de scandale*, also benefited from widespread interest among the public. On the agenda of the ultra-conservatives, this publication was happening at exactly the right time: it enabled them to increase their attacks on the Clinton administration, accused not only of wishing to protect minorities, but also to extend welfare and the rights which they count on.

Michael Joyce, the president of the Bradley Foundation, was able to claim that, in his view, Charles Murray was one of the most important social thinkers in the country – though certain people have pointed out that the mixture of pseudo-science and real racism bore a strange resemblance to the studies financed by the Pioneer Fund, an extreme right-wing organization that carried out research on eugenics.

The ideas in *The Bell Curve* spread with redoubtable effectiveness. Race, and the defence of the white race, implicitly became an ultra-conservative hobbyhorse. Gordon Lee Baum, the president of the Council of Conservative Citizens, extremely close to the leaders of the American Right, went so far as to declare that the overwhelming consensus among professionals and academics was that there was a difference in IQ between blacks and whites, and that *The Bell Curve* came close to the reality of the situation.[26]

In an interview he gave the *Washington Post*, Baum drove the lesson home: 'We're only 9 percent of the world's population, white Europeans, and our country's going to be majority nonwhite soon. Why can't European Americans be concerned with this genocide? Is that racial to say that?'[27] Baum had described Martin Luther King as a 'depraved miscreant'. His movement defended a return to racial segregation, the closing of borders to coloured immigrants, and attacks on interracial marriages; certain members even went as far as to support the Ku Klux Klan. This populist racism was supported by more subtle but just as dangerous remarks on the part of academics. So Ben Wattenberg, a researcher at the American Enterprise Institute, pondered this decline in population in the *New York Times Magazine*.

> The West has been the driving force of modern civilization, inexorably pushing towards democratic values. Will that continue when its share of the total [global] population is only 11 percent? Perhaps as less developed countries modernize, they will assimilate Western views. Perhaps the 21st will be another 'American century'. Perhaps not.[28]

George Bush's 'Breeding Ground'

The American Enterprise Institute (AEI) was to serve as a 'breeding ground' for George W. Bush when it came to drawing up his administration. The pillars of this organization were Richard Perle, one of the leading hawks; Irving Kristol, the main neo-conservative thinker, and father of William Kristol, the editor of the conservative magazine *Weekly Standard*; and Lynn Cheney.

The Vice-President's wife had described the television series *The Africans*, broadcast by the public channel PBS, as 'propaganda' since it portrayed the historical problems encountered by Africa as a consequence of colonial exploitation by Europeans.

Lynn Cheney militated to ensure that such programmes would no longer benefit from public financing. She had also warmly supported an article by Carol Iannone in the neo-conservative review *Commentary*, in which the author wrote that to award literary prizes as prestigious as the Pulitzer or the National Book Award to writers such as Toni Morrison or Alice Walker meant sacrificing 'the demand of excellence to the democratic dictatorship of mediocrity'.[29] While working at the AEI, Lynn Cheney also sat on the board of Lockheed Martin, the premier arms company.

In a book written in 1995, entitled *Telling the Truth*, Lynn Cheney attacked the philosopher Michel Foucault who claimed that truth was shaped by those in power. She wrote, 'If we are to be successful as a culture, we cannot follow Foucault and turn away from reason and reality. We must follow the great thinkers of the Enlightenment and find the will to live in truth ... The answer may very well determine whether we survive.'[30]

One of the other stars of the AEI is Dinesh D'Souza, who had arrived in the United States in 1978 with a Rotary scholarship. He became editor-in-chief of the *Dartmouth Review*, a conservative organ published by the college of the same name and financed by the Olin Foundation, and went on to edit the review of the Heritage Foundation, *Policy Review*, before becoming a political adviser for the Reagan administration. His first book, *Illiberal Education: The Politics of Race and Sex on Campus*, piled up anecdotes on the 'horrors' of the 'politically correct' and positive discrimination within universities. After moving to the AEI, he published in 1997 *The End of Racism*. His target: American blacks. According to the author, they must cease to use the 'excuse' of institutional racism to mask their failure to accomplish what whites and Asians successfully do, and to admit that they are sucked down by a 'culture of poverty', marked by an increased number of delinquents, illegitimate births, and total dependency on the welfare system and other government programmes.

D'Souza's observations, criticized by conservative blacks, though some of them were close to the AEI, came with radical proposals. The government should be held to 'a rigorous standard of colour-blindness, while allowing private actors to be free to discriminate as they wish'. According to D'Souza, 'individuals and companies would be allowed to discriminate in private transactions such as selecting a business partner or hiring for a job'. And, so that his objectives would be clearly understood and accepted, D'Souza declared, 'Am I calling for a repeal of the Civil Rights Act of 1964? Actually, yes.'[31]

The books by Charles Murray and Dinesh D'Souza were among the favourite reading matter of George W. Bush. But the thinker who has most delighted and persuaded him, and whose ideas became one of his favourite themes during the 2000 presidential campaign, is Marvin Olasky, the author of *The Tragedy of American Compassion*.

His book pleads in favour of an absolute dismantling of the American welfare system. Olasky, who became George W. Bush's adviser during his presidential campaign, forged the concept of 'conservative compassion' adopted by the President. He believes that poverty stems more from an absence of moral values than from the social inequalities of the current system. Olasky set up, in Austin, Texas, a church which teaches for instance that women have 'no place in leadership'.

Olasky's trajectory is a veritable deluge of successive commitments: a practising Jew, he abandoned Judaism, then atheism, to become an active member of the Communist Party before subscribing to the left-wing idealism of the 1960s. Today, a fanatical fundamentalist Christian, he remains a man who has the ear of the President, and is always ready to leap to his defence – as in the presidential campaign when he said he thought that the journalists who criticized George W. Bush had 'holes in their souls'.

4

Enter the Moonies

In 1981 the Reagan–Bush administration in Washington envisaged the creation of a big conservative daily newspaper in the federal capital, that could faithfully reflect its views and its political opinions, while at the the same time competing with the omnipresent *Washington Post*. That liberal bastion, bristling with an often excessive rigour and journalistic intransigence, constituted a real thorn in the flesh for the American Right.

They approached several potential sponsors, but all of them declined, even Richard Mellon Scaife, who hesitated for a long time before refusing. Admittedly, the challenge was considerable. The *Post*, part of a powerful press group including the magazine *Newsweek*, sells more than 800,000 copies a day in Washington and the District of Columbia. Any man crazy enough to take up the challenge could count on losing a lot of money over a long period of time. But the man who had launched the *Washington Times* in 1982, and whose offices were installed in the inner suburbs of Washington, did not have the reputation of being crazy – nor of being disinterested.

The man in question was the Reverend Sun Myung Moon, the founder in the 1960s of the Unification Church, considered to be a dangerous sect. From his innumerable declarations one could learn that he was the 'new Messiah', since Christ had failed in his mission, and that his objective was to unify the planet by gathering all its religious forces under his leadership.

In the 1970s Moon and his Church had been the subject of an inquiry into their activities on the part of a Congress commission led by the Democrat Representative Donald Fraser.

Moon had become a permanent resident of the United States in 1973, according to the reports of the Department of Justice, and his principal collaborator Bo Hi Pak, a former officer of the Korean CIA, affirms that he possessed a green card.

The organization of his empire, the many various societies that he controlled – several dozen of them in the United States alone – as well as his sources and channels of financing, were all surrounded by the most absolute secrecy. Except for the CIA. At the time Moon was being investigated by Congress, George Bush was the director of the intelligence agency. The CIA had been completely responsible for training the South Korean secret services (baptized KCIA), known for their redoubtable effectiveness against their Korean opponents abroad. Several of the latter had been kidnapped or executed.

Bush and his closest collaborators in the CIA considered South Korea as a 'highly sensitive' country for American national security, and the Reverend Sun Myung Moon as the pivot of clandestine actions undertaken jointly by the CIA and its Korean equivalent. The future president intervened personally with members of Congress to stop them from taking their investigations too far.[1] His efforts succeeded and Moon pledged his gratitude to George Bush – a gratitude that would be unfailing in the course of the next twenty-four years.

The guru of the Unification Church constantly mobilized his vast resources to favour the political ambitions of the Bush family. Father and son successively both benefited from the same largesse. But gratitude was not Moon's only motive. Thanks to the *Washington Times*, he was at the heart of American political power. He had spent more than 100 million dollars to launch a paper that was to become the favourite reading of the conservative establishment in Washington. Ronald Reagan stated that it was his 'favourite daily' and Vice-President Bush for his part declared that the *Times* was bringing reason and common sense to the federal capital. Despite these commendatory remarks, sales refused to take off and the *Washington Times* never became a real competitor to the *Post*. This commercial setback obliged Moon to inject several tens of millions of dollars every year to ensure the survival of his press organ.

This was a policy he had been practising since the beginning of the 1970s. In 1978 a Congressional Commission of Inquiry had looked into the scandal of 'Koreagate', a strategy implemented by the South Korean CIA designed to buy influence with the American government and other officials. Moon had been mentioned on several occasions as being involved in the operation, an accusation he had refuted.

The cleric had, however, made some quite unambiguous remarks to those around him. Allan Tatt Wood said Moon told him: 'Part of our strategy in the US must be to make friends in the FBI, the CIA and police forces, the military and business community'.[2] This was the case. The CIA regularly supplied the *Washington Times* with hitherto unpublished information and in return the paper launched violent counter-offensives when embarrassing information on sensitive topics was divulged.

During the period 1985–6, revelations emerged accusing the Contras, the anti-Sandinista rebels in Nicaragua supported by the Reagan–Bush administration, of being involved in drugs trafficking. The *Times* laid into the journalists and the Congressional investigators who were acting as the spokespersons and transmitters of these accusations. The response was so effectively organized that it silenced the rumours and succeeded in convincing the vast majority of Washington's political class that this information linking the Contras to drugs was not only false, but completely fabricated. These efforts came to nothing in 1988, when the Inspector General of the CIA acknowledged that several dozen Contra units were implicated in cocaine trafficking. He added that Ronald Reagan, Vice-President Bush and their close collaborators had taken pains to cover up the scandal.

The same year, George Bush entered the lists in his bid for the Presidency. Moon and the *Washington Times* resolutely lined up behind his candidacy. The Republican candidate, despite having occupied the post of Vice-President for eight years, claimed to be entirely unaware of the affairs and scandals that had broken out during the Reagan administration. And when the special prosecutor Lawrence Walsh, investigating Irangate, was just about to point the finger at George Bush, Moon's newspaper violently attacked him. He did not spare the Democratic opponent of the future president, Michael Dukakis, former Governor of Massachusetts, either, and circulated false rumours about his mental health. These insinuations contributed to undermining the credibility of Dukakis with public opinion and destabilizing his campaign.

The editor of the *Times*, and its editor-in-chief, Wesley Purden, had the advantage of direct and constant access to the White House when George Bush became the forty-first President of the United States. Inviting Purden to a private lunch, the President told him it was 'just to tell you how valuable the *Times* has become in Washington, where we read it every day'.[3]

'Our Father'

Flattering remarks, which illustrated the close links existing between the President and Moon. In 1992, when the President embarked on his fight for re-election, the *Times* echoed the rumours accusing his Democratic opponent, Bill Clinton, of having perhaps been recruited by the KGB during a trip to Moscow during his time as a Rhodes Scholar.

Anti-Communism was, in appearance, a powerful cement binding together Moon and the Republican administrations. But the reality was much more ambiguous. Moon, nicknamed 'Our Father' by his disciples, was actively financing South Korean political personalities, including two men: Kim Jong Pil, who was to occupy the post of Prime Minister in 1998 and 1999, and, in particular, the former opponent of the military regime, Kim Dae Jong, elected President in 1998 and a man who supported opening up dialogue with the North Korean Communist regime.

As early as 1991, when Pyongyang was still subject to a commercial embargo on the part of the United States and Bush Sr was still occupying the Oval Office, Moon sent the North Korean dictator Kim Il Sung several million dollars as a birthday present. The two men met several times, and the highly anti-Communist *Washington Times* had the signal honour of being given the first interview ever granted a Western capitalist newspaper by the last

Stalinist leader on the planet. According to information that came into the hands of the journalist Richard Perry based on reports drawn up by the DIA, the American military secret services, several meetings between the head of the sect and the Communist leader, held between 30 November and 8 December 1991, had allowed the bases of a commercial cooperation to be laid. The agreement made provision for the construction by Moon of a hotel complex in Pyongyang, the development of tourism in the Kimkangsan region, and investments in the Tumangang River zone, as well as the setting up of an electricity power station in Wonsan. These investments added up, according to the DIA, to a total of more than 3.5 million dollars.[4]

In 1993 the Unification Church sold land in Pennsylvania. The profits from the sale – approximately 3 million dollars, according to the DIA – passed via a Chinese bank to the Hong Kong subsidiary of the South Korean conglomerate Samsung. Shortly afterwards, the money was given to Kim Il Sung as a birthday present.[5]

Over and above the same authoritarian vision of the world, and a shared taste for absolute power, Moon and Kim had in common an unbridled yen for personality cults. The economic agreement reached with North Korea included a secret clause: in thanks for his help, Kim Il Sung granted the head of the Unification Church a concession of ninety-nine years, situated at Chongchu, Moon's birthplace. This zone was set apart to become a 'holy land', a place of pilgrimage on which all the Moonies from the entire world would converge.

This aid to the North Korean regime placed the Bush administration still in power in an embarrassing position. The American embargo on Pyongyang dated back to the time of the war between the two Koreas, at the start of the 1950s. It forbade any commercial or financial agreements 'between North Korea and any American citizen or permanent resident'.

This was precisely Moon's situation, officially residing as he was in Tarrytown, near New York. For numerous American officials, he had not only violated the laws, but supplied a dictatorship in dire straits with hard currency that it desperately needed, at the very time it was seeking to finance ambitious arms programmes.

Classified by George W. Bush among the countries of the 'axis of evil', North Korea had benefited twelve years earlier, as had Iraq, from his father's implicit support. With total impunity. Not only did George Bush not cause any difficulties for Moon, but the links between the two men grew even closer once he had left the Presidency in 1992.

George and Barbara Bush gave several lectures throughout the United States and Asia for organizations financed by Moon. In 1995, in Tokyo, they spoke in front of 50,000 people. The meeting was organized by the Women's Federation for World Peace, an association sponsored by Moon and presided over by Beverly LaHaye, an ultra-conservative Christian militant. Her husband Tim LaHaye, a Christian evangelist, is the author of the best-seller *Left Behind*, a religious fiction that sold in millions of copies, out-doing the best-sellers of John Grisham or Tom Clancy.

Tim LaHaye also created in 1981 another important organization that benefited from Moon's largesse, the Council for National Policy, and he had a seat on the board of the Religious Freedom Coalition, another association set up by Moon, which included several important members of the Christian ultra-Right, today close to George W. Bush.

In 1984 Moon had been imprisoned for fiscal fraud. He was given eighteen months in jail and a fine of 25,000 dollars. Tim LaHaye had at the time called on his supporters to join the Korean in prison, as a protest against this sentence.

In 1996 Moon decided to launch a new newspaper in Argentina, baptized *Tiempos del Mundo*, aiming to have it circulated in ten Latin American countries. At this time the man and his organization were the subject of intense criticism in the South American press. Attention was drawn to his supposed links with governments that had supported 'death squadrons', as well as with the Bolivian regime that had taken power after a putsch nicknamed the 'cocaine coup' because of the complicity between the political leaders and the drug traffickers.

The Argentinian President Carlos Menem's advisers were pushing him to boycott Moon's next visit. The influential Catholic Church talked of the veritable 'brainwashing' to which the Unification Church submitted its faithful, and reminded everyone that several countries, including Germany, considered Moon and his organization a threat to public order, and had refused him an entry visa.

100,000 Dollars for a Speech

The Reverend Sun Myung Moon arrived in Buenos Aires having successfully silenced all criticism. He brought with him the most respectable form of backing: George Bush in person, former president and star speaker at the evening event that had been organized.

Bush, who was received by President Menem, stayed at the official residence for foreign heads of state. Then, on 24 November at the Sheraton Hotel, in front of 700 hand-picked guests, he described Moon as a 'man of vision', before adding, in a burst of enthusiasm: 'The editors of the *Washington Times* tell me that never once has the man with the vision interfered with the running of the paper, a paper that in my view brings sanity to Washington DC. I'm convinced that *Tiempos del Mundo* is going to do the same thing.'[6]

The following day, Bush travelled with Moon to Uruguay, the neighbouring country, to inaugurate in his company in Montevideo a seminar that brought together 4,200 young Japanese people. The religious leader already owned a bank, a newspaper and a hotel in this country, and he had bought land in the province of Corrientes where he envisaged building 'ideal towns' for his disciples.

The former American President had been paid a very considerable amount for his speech in Buenos Aires, and one former leader of Moon's Unification Church suggests that the total earmarked for Bush's various activities amounted to many millions of dollars.[7] But as the newspaper of the brotherhood, *Unification News*, had written of the gala evening held in Buenos Aires: 'Mr Bush's presence as keynote speaker gave the event invaluable prestige. Father [Moon] and Mother [Mrs Moon] sat with several of the True Children [Moon's offspring] just a few feet from the podium.'[8] As a defender, with his wife, of 'true family values', George Bush had declared, with reference to one of the Moonie organizations, the Women's Federation for World Peace, 'Until I

see something about the Women's Federation that troubles me, I
will continue to encourage them'.[9]

But something ought to have been worrying the forty-first President of the United States for some considerable time: the violently
anti-American tone of the Reverend Sun Myung Moon's comments. The latter had, after all, declared: 'History will make the
position of Rev. Moon clear, and his enemies, the American people
and government, will bow down before him.'[10]

On 1 May 1997, in front of an audience of the faithful, he had
asserted, 'the country that represents Satan's harvest is America'.[11]

On 4 August 1996, three months before Bush's speech in
Argentina, Moon uttered these words: 'Americans who continue
to maintain their privacy and extreme individualism are foolish
people. Once you have this great power of love, which is big
enough to swallow entire America, there may be some individuals who complain inside your stomach. However, they will be
digested.'[12]

Nonetheless Bush, unperturbed, continued to cooperate with
a man who basically held him in low esteem, witness his comments reproduced on his website shortly after the election of
Bush Sr:

> Who is greater, President Bush or Reverend Sun Myung Moon?
> Why do you say Reverend Moon? My nose is wider, my eyes are
> smaller, and I am shorter than Mr. Bush. Also, Mr. Bush is white
> and I am a colored man. The United States is an advanced country
> while Korea is still developing. Reverend Moon's background is not
> so great and his support is not so powerful, while President Bush
> has the support of the whole country. But, strangely enough, many
> people in the world are saying, 'Reverend Moon is greater than Mr.
> Bush'. Why is that? It is because nobody else can take the place of
> Reverend Moon. Mr. Bush will be replaced by the next president,
> perhaps after just four years.[13]

As one important American magazine put it: 'Here is evidence
that Moon is openly anti-American and anti-democratic, with an
agenda that includes undermining American democracy and
individualism.'[14]

For years, he had tirelessly been using his great fortune and his taste for manipulation to win favours from conservative American leaders, both political and religious – the representatives of a country which, at bottom, he hated. The most piquant aspect of all this, apart from his cooperation with Bush, was the alliance he had woven with all the leaders of the Christian extreme Right, those intransigent defenders of America and its values. He had transformed them into his associates, and in some cases into his debtors.

At the end of 1993 the evangelist Jerry Falwell, leader of the Moral Majority, was experiencing grave financial difficulties. On 5 January 1994 he flew to Seoul, where he had a long meeting with the administrators of the Unification Church. Shortly afterwards he received 2.5 million dollars from Moon to bale out his university 'Liberty', situated in Virginia and on the verge of bankruptcy. Falwell later declared, 'If the American Atheists' Society or Saddam Hussein himself ever sent an unrestricted gift to any of my ministries, be assured I will operate on Billy Sunday's philosophy: "the Devil's had it long enough, and quickly cash the cheque".'[15]

Despite these remarks, Falwell had been won over, regularly speaking at demonstrations organized by Moon, showing respect and understanding for the 'new Messiah' and his sect. Falwell even went so far as to describe the Korean as 'an unsung hero to the cause of freedom who is to be commended for his determination, his courage and his endurance in support of his beliefs'.[16]

Falwell, who had supported the most defamatory campaigns launched against Bill Clinton, was not the only one to belong to the veritable 'network' set up by Moon. Tim LaHaye, the evangelist author of religious best-sellers, received 500,000 dollars from Bo Hi Pak, Moon's right-hand man and a former officer in the Korean CIA. A recording showed LaHaye thanking Bo for this payment. Ralph Reed, an official at the Heritage Foundation, Gary Bauer, executive director of the Christian Coalition and briefly a candidate for the presidential primaries, as well as Robert Schuller, a celebrated pastor and televangelist, also benefited from Moonie donations.

'A Biblical Vision of the World'

Sun Myung Moon had supporters from among the most extreme fringe of the Christian far Right. Speaking on the television show of his friend Pat Robertson, the founder of the Christian Coalition, Jerry Falwell had placed the blame for the attacks of 11 September not on terrorists, 'but on God, as retribution against homosexuals, civil libertarians and others on his enemies' list'.[17] Robertson himself thought that the tragedy of the World Trade Centre was the price to be paid for the immorality of a country – America – in which 40 million murders were committed. He was referring to abortions.[18]

These men were not at the head of small groups of cranks but of a significant electoral force, between 15 per cent and 18 per cent of voters, with powerful channels in the political world. No Republican candidate running for president could afford to ignore or disdain them. Moon – and this was the source of his strength – represented a real interface between politics and religion.

The Council for National Policy, set up in 1981 by the ultra-religious pastor and writer Tim LaHaye, benefited from his donations. And this organization, which functioned extremely discreetly, brought together all the emblematic figures of religious ultra-conservatism: Jerry Falwell and Pat Robertson, of course, but also Paul Weyrich of the 'Free Congress' and the creator of the Heritage Foundation, Phyllis Schlafly, a Christian political activist who claims that a woman's place is in the home; James Dobson, the mentor of George W. Bush, in charge of 'Focus on the Family', an organization and magazine centred on Christ; the Reverend James Robertson, one of the President's favourite televangelists; and Bob Jones III, who heads the ultra-conservative University of South Carolina named after him, and is well known for his openly anti-Catholic positions. Bob Jones describes the Pope as 'Antichrist'. His establishment received a controversial visit by George W. Bush during the 2000 presidential campaign. 'We had to send a message – fast – and sending him there was the only way to do it,' said one top Bush operative at the time. 'It was a risk we had to take.'[19]

On the political side, men as influential as Senator Jess Helms or Representatives Dick Armey, Howard Philips and Tom De Lay were members of this council. DeLay, elected in Texas, was in November 2002, after the victory of the Republicans in the House of Representatives, to become the most powerful man in Congress. Speaking in front of a group of religious representatives, he said, 'Only Christianity offers a way to live in response to the realities that we find in this world.'[20] He also stated that he had been entrusted with a divine mission – to promote 'a biblical worldview in American politics'.[21] For Joe Conason and Gene Lyons, the Council for National Policy (CNP) essentially 'functions as the central committee of a theocratic popular front'.[22] It is an alliance of individuals and groups which bury their differences to fight a common enemy. This enemy, defined in the abstract, is the separation enshrined in the American Constitution between Church and State. The most concrete targets of the CNP are liberals, various Democrats, and 'secular humanists' of every stripe, even including moderate Republicans. Numerous influential members of the CNP subscribe to a doctrine known as 'Christian reconstructivism'. This doctrine states that the essential legitimacy of the American Constitution derives from the Bible as it was interpreted by fundamentalist Protestants.

At the beginning of 1999, as the future presidential election was looming on the horizon, these religious groups were fully resolved, this time, to seize their opportunity and to gain power through a candidate who shared their views. They felt they had been treated too casually by the leaders of the Republican Party. Stated one observer, 'Their only power up until then had been to bring about the defeat of the official candidate. This had been the case in 1992 with Bush Sr., then in 1996 with Senator Bob Dole. In several messages they sent each other, they referred to the necessity, in the future, of "controlling the party".'[23]

'A Born-and-Bred Son of the Christian Right'

In 1999, one candidate seemed to have their preference – and it was not George W. Bush. His name was John Ashcroft and he came from the Deep South. Jeff Jacoby wrote in the *Washington*

Times that Ashcroft was 'a born-and-bred son of the Christian right'.[24] He could indeed point to an irreproachable career. He belonged to the Assemblies of God, the most important Pentecostal movement, with 2.3 million members in the United States, and more than 30 million adherents throughout the world. This was the first centralized religious institution to emerge from a Pentecostal movement that had developed at the start of the twentieth century in the United States.

His father was a minister in charge of the education branch in the governing body of the movement, based in Springfield, Missouri. Ashcroft became Governor, then Senator for Missouri: in December 1999 he told the religious magazine *Charisma*, 'It's said that we shouldn't legislate morality. Well, I think all we should legislate is morality. We shouldn't legislate immorality.'[25] Totally opposed to homosexuality, abortion (even if the woman is a victim of incest or rape), pornography, and . . . the United Nations, in the state of Missouri Ashcroft blocked the appointment of a judge whom he suspected of not being sufficiently in favour of applying the death sentence.

Systematically hostile to defendants, he nonetheless intervened to defend the case of Charles T. Sell, a St Louis dentist, accused by the Department of Justice of the attempted murder of an FBI agent and a witness, after he himself had been accused of medical fraud. It is true that Sell belonged to the conservative Citizens Council, an extreme right-wing organization that advocates the supremacy of the white race.

In his interventions, Ashcroft rewrites American and biblical history in a worrying and reductive way. Speaking in May 1999 at Bob Jones University in South Carolina, he stated that the American rebels who had risen up against the King of England had done so for religious reasons. 'Tax collectors came, asking for that which belonged to the King, and colonists frequently said, "We have no King but Jesus".'[26]

None of the founding documents of the American Revolution mentions Jesus and, in the Constitution, Church and State are rigorously separated. All the Founding Fathers, contrary to Ashcroft's claims, demonstrated a fierce hostility to an official Church of the kind that existed in England and certain other European countries.

His version of the episode of the Crucifixion is just as debatable.

Pilate stepped before the people in Jerusalem and said, 'Whom would ye that I release unto you? Barabbas? Or Jesus, which is called the Christ?' And when they said 'Barabbas', he said, 'But what about Jesus, King of the Jews?' And the outcry was, 'We have no king but Caesar'.[27]

As the journalist Robert Parry has emphasized, Ashcroft cannot even quote the Bible correctly. It was not the 'people of Jerusalem', but a few priests who replied in this way to Pilate. Such a distortion of the texts by a man of the church opened the door to the oldest slogans of anti-semitism: the Jewish people were collectively responsible for the death of Jesus.

To launch his presidential candidacy, Ashcroft received a gift of 10,000 dollars from the head of the Christian Coalition, Pat Robertson, and his wife. But in reality this was a Judas kiss. The President of the Christian Coalition had stated as early as 1992, 'We want . . . as soon as possible to see a majority of the Republican Party in the hands of pro-family Christians by 1996.'[28] Ashcroft was in no position to make a real impact on the national level and thus to fulfil this objective. On the other hand, Moon, with whom Robertson remained in close contact, was mobilizing in favour of the candidacy of George W. Bush. The *Washington Times* was embarking on a veritable sabotage operation to discredit the Democrat candidate Al Gore, Bill Clinton's Vice-President. One editorial was entitled 'Liar, Liar; Gore's Pants on Fire', and ended with these words: 'When Al Gore lies, it's without any apparent reason.'[29]

The Texas Governor, the elder son of the former president, possessed in Robertson's eyes two essential assets: considerable financial means, and close relations, which he carefully maintained, with all the fundamentalist Christian groups.

Robertson pushed the Christian Right to support George W. Bush and to eliminate his most dangerous adversary, Senator John McCain. Their electors later played a considerable role in the most closely fought states and in Florida, aided by the Federalist Society and its juridical networks, they swung the scales in Bush's favour. After the election they demanded, as the price of their support, the appointment of John Ashcroft to the post of Attorney General. The new President professed a great admiration for the former Missouri Senator and his views, but he envisaged for him a post as a judge in the Supreme Court.

Bush and Vice-President Cheney were then assailed by telephone calls from all the leaders of the religious Right, unanimously demanding the Department of Justice for Ashcroft. Their candidate also possessed one other major asset: ever since 1996, he had been the director of American Compass (compassion), an organization financed by Richard Mellon Scaife: its objective was to advocate religious commitment in the social sector. The other director of this institute was the aforementioned Marvin Olasky, the former Communist Jew who had become a fundamentalist Christian and adviser to George W. Bush.

Among fundamentalist Christians, 84 per cent had voted for Bush during the presidential elections. So Ashcroft became Attorney General.

Militant supporters of civic rights, environmental protection, and the constitutional separation of Church and State all demonstrated their indignation. The Christian Right and conservative juridical organizations did not conceal their satisfaction. Ashcroft controlled not only the judiciary, but also the FBI, the bureaux of alcohol, tobacco and firearms – all agencies with significant repressive powers at their disposal.

He also seemed to be on the same wavelength as a major section of political opinion. Polls revealed that a third of the postwar 'baby-boom' generation accepted the biblical idea that the world was created in seven days, thereby rejecting the theory of evolution, and considered that temptations were the work of the Devil.

For Pat Robertson and his Christian Coalition, who had made war on secularism their principal hobbyhorse, the spiritual confrontation could begin. 'There will be Satanic forces', he declared, before adding:

> The strategy against the American Radical Left should be the same as General Douglas MacArthur employed against the Japanese in the Pacific . . . Bypass their strongholds, then surround them, isolate them, bombard them, then blast the individuals out of their power bunkers with hand-to-hand combat. The battle for Iwo Jima was

not pleasant, but our troops won it. The battle to regain the soul
of America won't be pleasant either, but we will win it.[30]

Shortly after the new President's election, the Washington
Times Foundation, controlled by Moon, organized a lunch to cele-
brate this victory, at which were present Jerry Falwell, the evangelist Robert Schuller, Paul Crouch of the Christian Coalition, and
several other religious fundamentalists.

On 19 January 2001 a 'prayer breakfast' celebrating the beginning of George W. Bush's period of office took place at the Hyatt
Hotel in Washington. Moon received an award for his 'work in
support of traditional family values'.[31] The speaker was John
Ashcroft. The Attorney General, the tireless defender of American 'values', congratulated the man who explained to his disciples
that these same values were the work of Satan.

But the coming to power of this group also revived covetous
longings and led to solidarities fragmenting. Pat Robertson, at the
head of a personal fortune estimated at more than 150 million
dollars, partly invested in race horses, expressed reservations about
the 'Faith Based' programme announced by the President, which
offered public subsidies to churches' social and educational pro
grammes. Robertson anxiously noted that such a project could
benefit Moon.[32] The Korean is in fact trying to develop, with the
help of government funds, his sexual abstinence programmes in
state schools.

5

The Question of Israel

'The Jewish people in America and Israel and all over the world have no dearer friend than Jerry Falwell.'[1] The preacher and businessman Falwell never misses an opportunity to reaffirm the unstinting support of fundamentalist Christians for the Jewish state and Jewish communities. In 1985, during a banquet in Jerusalem that he was giving in honour of Moshe Arens, the Israeli Defence Minister and an important member of Likud, a witness heard the American lean towards the minister and tell him, 'I want to thank you for that jet plane you gave me.'[2] The Israeli government had presented him with a private jet in reward for the numerous services that he had rendered the State of Israel.

Falwell is one of the leaders belonging to the movement of 'Christian Zionists', as is Ed McAteer. At the age of 77, this former head of marketing at Colgate Palmolive counts as one of the main coordinators of that extremely well-organized and highly determined lobby that no American political leader can afford to ignore. McAteer embarked on this militant activism in 1976, at a time when many conservative Christian groups were expressing openly anti-semitic opinions and making no secret of their links with extreme right-wing racist organizations such as the Ku Klux Klan and the John Birch Society.

For more than twenty years now, Zionist Christians and government leaders have been working 'hand in hand', in the words of McAteer, a born-again Christian like George Bush who likes to say, 'The best friends that Israel has are those people who believe the Bible does not contain the word of God but that the Bible is the word of God.'[3]

Ever since the middle of the twentieth century, the term 'fundamentalist' has characterized an extremely aggressive and intransigent form of Protestantism, insisting on the struggle against cultural decadence and liberal theology. This movement considers that the world and mankind are God's creations, and frequently refers to the celebrated trial brought in 1925 against Scopes, a biology teacher in Tennessee who was teaching his pupils the theory of evolution – something which for fundamentalists is the height of horror and absurdity.

Even more worryingly, several of these movements subscribe to the predictions of John Darby. This nineteenth-century pastor considered that a series of events would announce the last days of our world. These early warning signs are war, the appearance of a new political and economic world order, and finally the return of the Jews to the Promised Land promised to Abraham.

The Battle of Armageddon

Darby developed a doctrine, baptized 'dispensionalism', popularized by the religious novels written by the ultra-conservative pastor and friend of Moon, Tim LaHaye.

According to Darby's prophecies, God turned away from Israel which had rejected the Messiah to create, construct, and miraculously evacuate the church before the great tribulation. Several phases will precede this end of the world. During the 'rapture', 'true believers will join Christ in the air'.[4] The 'tribulation' will mark the arrival of Antichrist, who will take over power throughout the world: an episode marked by the Battle of Armageddon before the second return of Christ and the establishment of the Kingdom of God.

This happy ending depends on the conversion of the Jews. And this cannot take place unless the Jews are in possession of all the lands that God gave them. In other words – as Matthew Engel of the *Guardian* has put it – these Christians only support the Jews so as to abolish them. Jerry Falwell, of course, but also Pat Robertson and D. L. Moody, the founder of the Moody Bible Institute, subscribe to this doctrine, as does Michael Geerson, the man who writes the speeches of George W. Bush, and whose office in the White House is the one closest to that of the President.

As Stan Crock remarked in *Business Week*, 'From the days of Saladin, a medieval Islamic ruler, to the Ottoman Empire, and now to the era of Saddam Hussein, Christian fundamentalists have viewed Islamic leaders as a possible Antichrist or its forerunner.'[5] And he went on to note, as he examined the theories of John Darby, that after seven years of Satanic domination, Christ and his saints – probably represented by George W. Bush and his collaborators – will return and triumph over evil during the Battle of Armageddon, an ancient battlefield near Haifa in the north of Israel. Once established in Jerusalem, Christ will reign peacefully for a thousand years, the 'millennium' so fervently awaited by these believers.

This interpretation of the Bible finds powerful politicians to relay it. Just like John Ashcroft, Tom DeLay, a Representative from Texas, now the most powerful man in Congress, shares these views. During the second Palestinian intifada, DeLay, who nonetheless is one of his friends, warned Bush and his administration in clear terms against any attempt to exert pressure on Ariel Sharon to obtain the withdrawal of Israeli troops from the West Bank. 'We should support Israel as they dismantle the Palestinian leadership that foments violence and fosters hate,' he declared at the University of Fulton, Missouri, the place where Winston Churchill had in 1946 made his famous speech on the 'iron curtain' that symbolically marked the beginning of the Cold War.[6]

'If you just focus on the power of Jewish [lawmakers] and Jewish groups in forming US policy on Israel, you're missing the boat. The Christian right has had a real influence in shaping the views of the Republican Party toward Israel,' says Steven Spiegel, Professor of Political Science at the University of California.[7]

The reality probably lies somewhere in the middle.

Israel's lightning victory during the Six Days' War in 1967, and the conquest of the whole of Jerusalem, had unleashed huge excitement among the 'dispensionalists' who subscribe to Darby's ideas. Nelson Bell, the editor of *Christianity Today* and the father-in-law of the celebrated preacher Billy Graham, had written in July 1967, 'That for the first time in more than 2,000 years

Jerusalem is now completely in the hands of the Jews gives the student of the Bible a thrill and a renewed faith in the accuracy and validity of the Bible.'[8]

This enthusiasm needs to be somewhat qualified. Billy Graham, now in his eighties, has acted as confessor and counsellor to over half a dozen American presidents. The only real written trace of his remarks, and his thoughts, are the retranscriptions of those notorious tapes in which he conversed with Richard Nixon. We have already mentioned his comments about the 'domination of the Jews over the [American] media', but in the course of another discussion with the President in the White House, he remarked, 'A lot of the Jews are great friends of mine. They swarm around me and are friendly to me because they know that I'm friendly with Israel. But they don't know what I really feel about what they are doing to this country.'[9] The televangelist Pat Robertson, for his part, had referred in a book written in 1990 to the corrosive effect of the 'liberal Jewish population' on American public life.

Graham has publicly apologized for these remarks, but an anecdote related by George W. Bush to Sam Howe Verhoek of the *New York Times* is illuminating. Bush, in conversation with his mother, asserted that only Christians would go to heaven. Barbara Bush telephoned to Billy Graham to ask his opinion. Graham replied to Bush that he agreed with him personally, but advised him not to play at God.[10]

This ambiguous alliance between Israel and conservative Christians was established in 1977 when Menachem Begin and Likud, the party of the Israeli Right, first came to power. For Begin, it was a question of blocking at all costs the initiatives of President Jimmy Carter, who wished to launch negotiations that would lead to the recognition of the right of Palestinians to their own country. Likud endeavoured to bring these fundamentalists over onto the same side as the Christian ultra-conservatives who supported Israeli intransigence. Carter thereby found himself deprived of an important electoral base.

Full-page advertisements, bought in the main American newspapers, declared, 'The time has come for evangelical Christians to affirm their belief in biblical prophecy and Israel's divine right to the land.' Targeting Soviet involvement in the UN conference, the ads went on to say, 'We affirm as evangelicals our belief in the promised land to the Jewish people. . . . We would view with grave concern any effort to carve out of the Jewish homeland another nation or political entity.'[11]

Sharon, a Rock Star

In 1980, the massive support given by Zionist Christians to Ronald Reagan was one of the reasons for Jimmy Carter's defeat. In June 1981 Menachem Begin telephoned Jerry Falwell, even before he called the American President, just after he had ordered the destruction of the Iraqi nuclear power station in Osiraq. And when in 1982 Begin's government decided to invade the Lebanon, the main architect of this intervention, Ariel Sharon, the then Defence Minister, went to the United States to ensure he had the support of the conservative Christians.

Ariel Sharon's appearances before Zionist Christians won him ovations normally reserved, according to one witness, for rock stars.[12] The Israeli Prime Minister in any case holds a special place. For certain extremists of the 'dispensionalist' doctrine, Sharon is the man chosen by God to accomplish the prophecies announcing the end of the world. They refer to his itinerary: he experienced power and then disgrace for his alleged role in the massacres at Sabra and Shatila. And they base their view on this quotation from the Bible: 'For a just man falleth seven times, and riseth up again' (Proverbs 24: 16).

This support given to Israel for theological reasons is based on a literal interpretation of the Bible. In supporting the 'Greater Israel' programme defended by Begin and Likud, which provides for the annexation of the territories occupied since 1967, Christian Zionists claim that they are merely responding to God's summons as it is formulated in the Old Testament.

Matthew Engel, writing in the *Guardian* on 28 October 2002, described the annual gathering of the Christian Coalition of America. This was attended by thousands of people, all cheering for Israel and for the speakers on the platform: amongst them, an Israeli student, followed by the mayor of Jerusalem Ehud Olmert.

The oddity is that few in the audience actually seemed to be Jewish, at least not in the conventional sense. Support for Israel's claim to the entire Holy Land was being enthusiastically offered by thousands of non-Jewish people. Weekly church attendance in the USA stands at about 40 per cent – against 2 per cent in the UK – and the relationship between religion and politics is strong. When Bush was deciding on his Middle East policy, he was influenced by both the Jewish lobby and the Christian 'religious conservatives'. As Matthew Engel wrote:

> A decade ago, when the President's father was in the White House, his eldest son's election-time job was to act as unofficial ambassador to this group, offer assurances that they and the administration were at one on such matters as abortion and pornography and prayer in schools, the issues they like to group together as 'family values'.

Opposition to a Palestinian state comes not only from the Christian Right, but also from

> anti-Zionist Hasidic Jews from Brooklyn in long black coats, who oppose the state of Israel based on their own reading of the Bible.
> . . .
> You might think these Christian activists represent the furthest shores of American politico-religious wackiness. The politicians don't think so. This conference began with a videotaped benediction straight from the Oval Office. Some of the most influential republicans in Congress addressed the gathering including – not once, but twice – Tom DeLay, who is hot favourite to take over as majority leader of the House of Representatives after the midterm elections on November 5, thus becoming arguably the most powerful man on Capitol Hill.

The secret agenda behind the support of the Christian Right for Israel, that Jews should ultimately be converted, was not something that speakers at the gathering are prepared to admit. The Jewish leaders, meanwhile, were prepared to accept this support if it would help them in their battle over Israel. Meanwhile, as Engel remarks, 'The linkage between the Christian Right and the Republican Party is getting ever stronger, especially in the electorally crucial states of the south and west', making it easier for the President to appoint right-wingers to all three branches of government in Washington.[13]

William Cook clearly summarizes the surrealism of these positions when he writes, 'Is it possible to believe in the 21st century that a God, designed by a small tribe of nomadic Semites 3,500 years ago . . . could dictate to Americans how they should conduct foreign policy?'[14]

The Antichrist is 'Jewish and Male'

During the 2000 presidential election, George Bush had won only 19 per cent of votes of the Jewish electorate as a whole, traditionally inclined as it is to vote Democrat. But the outbreaks of violence that had flared up in the Palestinian zones had tightened the alliance between conservative Christians and Jewish supporters of Israel even more. Shortly after the events of 11 September, the American President had reaffirmed his support and his understanding for the struggle against terrorism led by Ariel Sharon. This position corresponded to the profound convictions of the incumbent in the White House, but it also spelled out precious electoral gains for him.

The polls carried out by his strategist, Karl Rove, indicated that the voting intentions of the Jewish electorate in favour of Bush increased considerably in key states such as Florida, Michigan and Pennsylvania. New York, a traditional Democratic bastion, was showing a majority of Jewish votes favourable to the Republican President. For James M. Hutchens, the President of 'Christians for Israel', 'While Jewish votes assure that New York's Senators will always be demonstrably pro-Israel, those votes cannot begin to explain the broad consensus of congressional support for Israel and the consistently positive feeling toward Israel. Many of Israel's staunchest supporters in Congress have traditionally come from states with small Jewish populations'.[15]

Even if this administration shared their views, the Zionist Christians maintained a constant vigilance and pressure on its policies. The majority leader in the House of Representatives, Tom DeLay, as firm and constant in his unconditional support to Sharon as he was in his criticisms of Arafat, had pushed through a vigorously pro-Israeli resolution.

William Kristol, a Jewish neo-conservative thinker, close to George W. Bush and the Pentagon hawks Richard Perle and Paul Wolfowitz, wrote in his magazine *Weekly Standard*, 'We think you can't have a peace process in which one of the partners is a sponsor of terrorism. Not if you're engaged in a serious war on terrorism.'[16]

This position was completely shared by the Zionist Christians. Garry Bauer, the president of American Values and a pillar of the ultra-conservative religious establishment, had in June 2002 sent an open letter to the American President, co-signed by several leaders of the Christian Right, including Jerry Falwell, saying, 'We would ask you to end pressure on Israeli Prime Minister Ariel Sharon so that he has the time necessary to complete the mission he has undertaken – the elimination of terrorist cells and infra-structure from the West Bank territories.'[17] The former head of the Christian Coalition, Ralph Reed, declared for his part that there was, at present, no greater proof of God's sovereignty over the world than the survival of the Jews and the existence of Israel. Hence, he added, the firmness of the support given to Israel by Christians and other conservatives who shared their faith.

In 1998, when Benyamin Netanyahu, the then Israeli Prime Minis-ter, had gone to Washington, his first meeting had not been with Bill Clinton but with Jerry Falwell and more than 1,000 fundamental-ist Christians gathered for the occasion. That same year, in the course of a convention of the Christian extreme Right, he had caused a considerable stir by violently attacking the American President. Since the start of the 1990s, Netanyahu had exploited his post as the Israeli ambassador to the UN to establish close links with the leaders of the Christian Right. After Ariel Sharon's election as Prime Minister, the cooperation became even closer. The Israeli ambassador to Washington very regularly invites the leaders and main executives of these Christian organizations so that he and they can together coordinate their actions.

It is an ambiguous alliance, since Christian support rests more on their belief in the biblical prophecies than on any respect for

Jews and Judaism. As Ken Silverstein and Michael Sherer wrote in *Mother Jones*: 'They work to support Israel, ironically, because they believe it will lead to the ultimate triumph of Christianity. For them, the on-going crisis in the Mideast has been prophesied in the Bible.'[18]

Gershom Gorenberg in the *International Herald Tribune* on 14 October 2002 said, 'The Christian right's view of Israel derives largely from a double-edged theological position. Following the classic anti-Jewish stance it regards the Jewish people as spiritually blind for rejecting Jesus.'[19] Jerry Falwell, a great ally of Likud and the Israeli leaders, affirmed that the Antichrist has already arrived and that he is 'Jewish and male'. For the pastor Chuck Mussler, 'Auschwitz was just a prelude to what will happen in the approaching Armageddon.'[20]

However, in December 2002 Sharon, addressing 1,500 Zionist Christians, declared that he considered them to be Israel's best friends in the whole world.

This alliance between the Bush administration and the current Israeli government cannot conceal the disquieting way in which Darby's ideas have been taken up by these extremist Christians: at the end of Armageddon, that final battle between good and evil, many Jews will convert to Christianity, and the unbelievers, including Jews and Muslims, will perish and be damned. The Messiah will then lead the just into Paradise.

W. A. Criswell, the head of the biggest Baptist church in Dallas, Texas, publicly asked, 'Does God Almighty hear the prayers of Jews?' His response was unambiguous and peremptory: 'No'.[21] Bailey Smith, a former president of the Southern Baptist Church, echoes his views: according to him, 'God does not hear the prayers of the Jews.'[22]

On 10 February 2003 George W. Bush presided over the national convention of religious broadcasters in Nashville, Tennessee. In front of a crowd that applauded him thunderously, he was presented by the organizers as 'our friend and brother in Christ'.[23] In his role as Commander-in-Chief of his country, the President gave a speech in which international, domestic and economic problems were perceived and referred to in spiritual terms. 'I welcome faith,' he began. 'I welcome faith to help solve the nation's deepest problems.'[24] The spectators present punctuated each pause in his address with approving cries of 'Amen!'

The Weight of the Deep South

America is experiencing a strange swing of the pendulum. For decades, the presidents who succeeded each other in the White House came from the East Coast. Then, starting with the Texan Lyndon Johnson in 1963, there was a slide to the west: Nixon, Reagan, Bush Sr. With George W. Bush, the country's centre of gravity became the long-neglected Deep South. Bush had lived and grown up in Midland, Texas, but his faith, his strict religious attitude, without subtlety or compromise, is that of the inhabitants of the Southern States composing the Bible Belt. For the first time in the history of the United States, this Deep South is playing a decisive role in the conduct of the country's affairs. Men such as John Ashcroft, the Attorney General, and numerous extremist or fanatical religious leaders close to power, all come from this region.

This South also plays an extremely important role in the war mentality and the reinforcing of the notorious industrial–military complex, both supported by the powers that be in Washington. As the magazine *Counter Punch* explains, while the South represents only a third of the population of America, it includes 42 per cent of its soldiers. Of the troops based on American soil 56 per cent are in the South, and Congressional members from the southern states tend to be more hawkish than the rest. Not only does the South produce more arms than any other region (over 43 per cent of all arms contracts signed in the US), over two-thirds of the American weapons used by Israel are made in factories that the arms producers possess in the South.[25]

Le Monde, in an article by Henri Tincq, pointed out that American missionaries, during the war, were already camping at the gates of Iraq, 'ready to fly to the help, both "material and spiritual", of the population once it is "liberated" from Saddam Hussein. The Baptist Convention of the South and Samaritan Purse, a humanitarian association led by Franklin Graham, son of the famous televangelist Billy Graham, already have teams at the frontier with Jordan.'[26] Franklin Graham, who had the privilege of 'blessing' the ceremony of George W. Bush's swearing in, in January 2001, and who is regularly invited to the White House, has regularly distinguished himself by his violent diatribes against Islam: 'The God of Islam is not the same God. He's not the Son of God of the Christian or Judeo-Christian faith.'[27] It is hardly necessary to point out that 90 per cent of Iraqis are Muslims.

6

Hawks and Doves

The forces of the Christian extreme Right in America are not the only ones at work in the Bush administration. Certain elements of the presidential team, among the most outspoken in their support for the operation 'Iraqi Freedom', set out ideas that are in every detail similar to those of their fundamentalist counterparts, without, however, subscribing to their views and their vision of the world. They are Jews, close to the Israeli Likud and supporters of strong-armed tactics when it comes to the Palestinian problem.

Since Bush came to power, and even more since 11 September 2001, these men have earned an astonishing closeness to the Commander-in-Chief of the premier army in the world, who lends an attentive ear to their recommendations and their views. They are behind the new American foreign policy, based on interventionism and force – a surprising philosophy in this President, who was incapable of naming five different heads of state during a television broadcast a few weeks before the elections.

But the relations that link them to Israel and to part of the entire political class of that country pose serious questions both about the ethics and the validity of their actions. Douglas Feith, the Under-Secretary of State at Defense, constitutes a typical example of this inextricable intimacy between the current administration and the Israeli Right. Feith is thus very close to the Zionist Organization of America (ZOA), where he delivers many speeches. This organization, as influential as it is radical, rewarded his father Dalck, who was a member of Betar (a fanatical splinter group castigated by almost the entirety of the Jewish world community).

Before taking up his post, Douglas Feith was the head of a law firm which had foreign bureaux only in Israel. The Under-Secretary of Defense is not the only hawk in Washington to have connections with Israel. It is known, for example, that Richard Perle, another person influential among those who are today described as neo-conservatives, has worked for the Soltam firm, which manufactures artillery pieces and mortars (a row of shells holds pride of place on the first page of their website, which refers to 'battle-proven solutions').[1]

However, Douglas Feith possesses one particularity which is found in neither Perle nor in any other of his associates: he is the only American leader to hold Israeli bonds. This is a negligible investment for the Under-Secretary of Defense, as he is – and this is inevitably the case with those in the current administration – at the head of a considerable fortune: over 27 million dollars.

Again before his arrival at the Pentagon, Feith was also the director of the Center for Security Policy, a research organization where, yet again, moderation is hardly the order of the day. The CSP itself summarizes its doctrine in these terms: 'Promoting peace through strength.'[2]

This centre was for a long time directed by a man called Frank Gaffney, who constitutes a traditional conduit between the Christian Zionists of the American ultra-right and the Israeli hawks. He has always been considered to be one of the fiercest supporters of Benyamin Netanyahu and Ariel Sharon in the United States. On 17 December 2001 he declared to a gathering in a luxury hotel in Washington, including Douglas Feith, Donald Rumsfeld and Richard Perle, 'It's taken us 13 years to get here, but we've arrived.'[3] An allusion to the hawks who were now in power . . .

Moving in the same circles, in the same strongly conservative research centres that in particular are well disposed to the Israeli Right, Richard Perle is a totally atypical figure in American politics, or in politics anywhere, for that matter. Nicknamed, during the Reagan years, 'the Prince of Darkness', Perle likes nothing less than to be in the limelight. He aspires to no official post (at the time of the appointment of Pentagon officials, numerous observers were surprised not to see him there). Perle wants power, influence, and discretion. As one highly placed official put it, 'Perle is living what we all dream of in Washington: he has access to the most confidential material, and can influence decisions without ever having to explain himself.'[4] Of all the hawks, he is the one who has the most decisive influence, with Paul Wolfowitz. Perle directed the Defense Policy Board, a think tank and research group dependent on the Pentagon, with no direct power of decision-making. Following the financial scandals that I will be referring to later, he was forced to stand down from his post, but he nonetheless remains a member of the group. However this may be, any official post he holds is unimportant, insofar as Washington's current foreign policy reflects his writings to the letter. The 'Prince of Darkness' is more powerful than ever.

He too is a fierce defender of Israel. His whole career attests to the fact. Perle earned his spurs in the team of the Democratic Senator Henri 'Scoop' Jackson. Furthermore, he boasts, even now, of being a member of the Democratic Party, in memory of his mentor. That senator, who died almost twenty years ago, probably contributed more than anyone to shaping today's hawks (it is interesting to note that Wolfowitz and Feith have also worked in Jackson's team). 'Harder' than most of the Republicans of that time, Jackson pushed his team to fight on all fronts, combating all the arms reduction treaties that were presented to Congress. They managed to block the ratification of the Salt 2 treaty for the non-proliferation of nuclear weapons, before the Soviet invasion of Afghanistan definitively buried the project. More significantly, Jackson (and his team) was at the heart of the negotiations which later allowed Jewish emigrants from the Soviet Union to go to Israel. The Senator had insisted, by means of an amendment which bears his name, on imposing commercial sanctions on Moscow until arrangements to make their emigration possible had been ensured.

The School of Force

Perle and his comrades learnt in this school that force allowed one to achieve one's ends. That its use, or the mere threat of its use, was morally acceptable if its served just causes. Ratifying treaties of nuclear non-proliferation with the Soviet enemies constituted an avowal of weakness, especially when that very same enemy was starting to weaken. Later events justified him. And reinforced even more the convictions that he holds today: when faced with an intractable enemy, good can triumph only through force.

Perle's career ran into its first hitch when rumours stemming from the NSA (National Security Agency) accused him of having divulged confidential documents to Israel. He is very close both to Israel and to one of the directors of the Hollinger Corporation, which owns in particular the daily newspaper the *Jerusalem Post* and until recently owned the London *Daily Telegraph*.

Wolfowitz is only apparently different from Perle: the one stays in the background, the other occupies a prominent post in the American defence apparatus. But their paths have continually crossed over the last thirty years – in particular at the JINSA, the Jewish Institute for National Security Affairs, a think tank and source of support for Israel, whose aim is to 'inform the American Defense and Foreign Affairs Community about the important role Israel can and does play in bolstering democratic interest in the Mediterranean and Middle East'.[5]

But the JINSA is in fact a pressure group whose objectives are twofold: to block hi-tech arms sales to the Arab world, and to maintain an uninterrupted flow of American military assistance to the State of Israel. In their documents, one can read, for example:

> THE UNITED STATES must remain committed to maintaining Israel's technological edge both for America's sake as well as for the sake of Israel. Their security interests are linked by the fact that Israel is the most important democracy in this region of volatile dictatorships and unstable governments. The U.S. must be cognizant of its and Israel's security needs when deciding to sell advanced weapons to the Arab world, making technology transfers and when monitoring and reacting to transfers from third party sources.[6]

Today, with Paul Wolfowitz and Douglas Feith in the Pentagon, this advice may well gain a hearing.

Another key player is Elliott Abrams. Appointed in December 2002 to head the Middle East division at the National Security Council, under Condoleezza Rice, he led the hawks into particularly muddy waters that the group would probably far rather have avoided. Abrams is a man of religion. Not the most religious person in this administration, since the Pentagon's Chief Financial Officer, Dov Zackheim, is an orthodox rabbi who taught in the New York yeshiva. But Abrams nonetheless explains, in one of his books, that the Jews must safeguard their identity in America, not by focusing on blood ties, but rather by assiduously practising religious rituals.

Shortly after Ariel Sharon came to power, he published an article in which he explained that 'years of American pressure on Israel that have coincided with winking in Arafat's direction, and ignoring [Palestinian] violations of the agreement that they have signed, must come to an end'.[7]

In a remark aimed at those who criticize Israeli policies towards these very same Palestinians, Abrams declares that they are forgetting that the State of Israel is the 'only democracy' in this region, and that it is surrounded by 'ganglands activities'.[8] This man, in charge of the Middle East division at the National Security Council, is the same one who composes, endorses or blocks reports on the Israeli–Palestinian conflict, before they get as far as Condoleezza Rice or George Bush.

Before taking office, Abrams presided over the US Commission on International Religious Freedom, with the responsibility for inspecting the countries where freedom of worship was not respected. Here is the evidence of Dr Al Marayati, a member of that commission:

> In the spring of 2001, the Commissioners decided that a trip to the Middle East was in order, agreeing to include Egypt and Saudi Arabia in view of the discrimination against religious minorities, particularly Christians, in those countries. Because the Commission had also addressed discrimination in Israel against Muslims, Christians and non-Orthodox Jews in previous meetings, naturally Israel would be added to the itinerary. As Chairman of the Commission at the time, Abrams led the delegation to Egypt and Saudi Arabia, but did not go to Jerusalem with three of us as he was of the opinion that there are no problems with religious freedom in Israel that would warrant the attention of the Commission.
>
> A brief look at the Country Reports on Human Rights published annually by the State Department reveals that the degree of dis-

crimination against minorities in Israel proper (not to mention the
Occupied Territories) is at least on a par with if not worse than
that experienced by Coptic Christians in Egypt. . . . Ultimately,
under the leadership of Abrams, the Commission published reports
on over a dozen countries, including those visited throughout the
year, except for Israel.[9]

Elliott Abrams is a hardliner, an ultra-radical supporter of
inflexibility when it comes to putting an end to what he sees as
Israel's intractable enemy: the Palestinian Authority. It is interesting to note that he was also a member of 'Scoop' Jackson's team
in the 1970s, in company with Perle, Feith and Wolfowitz.

The Gladiator

Unlike his former colleagues, Abrams was implicated in particularly shadowy and nauseating affairs. As an assistant to the
Secretary of State under Reagan, he was one of the architects of
American policy in Latin America. He depicted himself as the
'gladiator' of Reagan's doctrine in this region, generously financing
the anti-Communist 'armies' which sometimes committed the
worst atrocities with America's blessing, especially in El Salvador.
    Abrams even denied that, as was later confirmed, a massacre
had taken place in the village of El Mozote, explaining that this
was just 'Communist propaganda'. After a United Nations commission of inquiry had examined the 22,000 or so atrocities committed during the twelve years of civil war, and after this same
commission had concluded that a great majority of the brutalities
had been committed by pro-American forces, Abrams declared
that 'The Administration's record on El Salvador is one of fabu-
lous achievement!'[10] Calling his enemies 'vipers', he stated that
any Congress members who blocked aid to the anti-Communist
militia of Latin America would have 'blood on their hands' – El
Salvador, but also Guatemala, Nicaragua and Angola. Abrams
was accused of having covered up numerous human rights
violations during the blackest operations carried out in the history
of the United States.

After he was found guilty of not having divulged the information required by Congress on his activities in Central America, accused of perjury during the Iran–Contra affair, then pardoned by the father of the current President in 1992, many suspect George W. Bush of having placed him under Condoleezza Rice so as to avoid having to ask for endorsement from the Senate: appointments within the National Security Council are the only ones that can be decided unilaterally by the President.

According to the *New York Times* of 7 December 2002, which quotes an official of the Bush administration, 'Mr Abrams' ascension had created "serious consternation" at the State Department. It was seen there, he said, as likely to impede the efforts of Secretary of State Colin L. Powell to work with European nations to press Israel and the Palestinians to adopt a staged timetable leading to creation of a Palestinian state in three years.'[11]

But this reticence did not embarrass the President. As Senator Charles Shummer (NY) explained, again in the *New York Times*, 'There are two foreign policy teams in this administration on a lot of issues . . . Clearly Elliott is coming out of the hard-line team. But that is where Bush's heart is.'[12]

Questioned on 4 December 2002, the spokesperson of the White House, Ari Fleischer, declared:

> Obviously, he was hired by this administration because of the outstanding work he has done for our country. And I think if you take a look, particularly in Latin and Central America, at nations that were not governed by democracies, and the advent of democracy that swept Latin and Central America in the '80s and throughout the '90s, Elliott Abrams played a very important role in that. And we are honored and pleased to have him work here at the White House.[13]

This same Ari Fleischer cannot be considered as one of the pillars of the neo-conservative network. He is not classified among the hawks – perhaps because his work, with its permanent contact with the press, imposes a certain restraint on him – and neither is he a direct sympathizer with the Israeli Likud. In fact, Ari Fleischer has gone much further.

The spokesperson of the White House has been the Co-President of Chabad's Capitol Jewish Forum, organized by the sect of the Chabad Lubavitch Hasidics. The Lubavitch are disciples of the Kabbala; they represent a branch of Judaism which most Israelis, even in Likud, would like to see fade away. Here is one example of the remarks made by Rabbi Menachem Schneerson, the leader of the Orthodox Chabad movement:

> 'Let us differentiate.' Thus, we do not have a case of profound change in which a person is merely on a superior level. Rather, we have a case of 'let us differentiate' between totally different species. This is what needs to be said about the body: the body of a Jewish person is of a totally different quality from the body of [members] of all nations of the world . . . A non-Jew's entire reality is only vanity. It is written, 'And the strangers shall guard and feed your flocks' (Isaiah 61: 5). The entire creation [of a non-Jew] exists only for the sake of the Jews.[14]

Ari Fleischer also received the Young Leadership Award of the American Friends of Lubavitch, in October 2001. The event was related in an article in the *Baltimore Jewish Times* in these terms:

> Like that of most high-ranking White House officials, the life of press secretary Ari Fleischer has become exhausting after the 11 September terrorist attacks. But he took a few hours off last week to pick up an award from American Friends of Lubavitch, and to help boost the group's extensive Jewish outreach efforts on Capitol Hill – efforts that Mr Fleischer, a former congressional staffer, has supported from the beginning.[15]

Assad 'Worse' than Saddam

Neo-conservatives do not represent the entirety of the Jewish and Israeli community, far from it. Just a small group of men pursuing objectives that they alone have defined, by means which they increasingly have sole control over, and whose influence in this administration continues to grow. A man like Fleischer does not belong to these groups, but his contacts with a racist, ultra-religious and fiercely anti-Arab movement shows the extent to which the American executive is today under their influence. And these are men who reach their decisions in Washington, and who think they are working for the good of a country, Israel, where they do not live, by applying policies which often go against the deep aspirations of the Israeli people, subject as they are to war and terrorism. The ideas of the hawks find an effective sounding board in the ministerial cabinets of Likud, but less of one in the streets of Tel Aviv, where peace is desperately longed for.

In addition, their growing power no longer seems to encounter any resistance within the administration. The more 'multilateralist' and moderate approach of Colin Powell, the declared opponent of the hawks, seems on the verge of purely and simply passing away. The Pentagon was 'purged' at the end of 2001 of its last dove, Bruce Reidel, who had suggested maintaining a wider coalition in the war against terrorism and paying heed to Arab susceptibilities that might be ruffled by a possible attack on Iraq.

So as to isolate Colin Powell completely, Wolfowitz and Rumsfeld succeeded in imposing on him another character who had totally fallen in with the ideas of the hawks: despite the hesitations of the Secretary of State, John Bolton was appointed Under-Secretary of State for Arms Control and International Security. He is the vice-president of the American Enterprise Institute, another research group with which the same men, yet again, cooperate, including Richard Perle and Douglas Feith; he is also the author of an article that appeared in the neo-conservative review *Weekly Standard*, edited by William Kristol, in which he sets out in detail his vision of the UN, one that is the complete opposite of Colin Powell's. On the subject of Kofi Annan, who tries to limit conflicts and to advocate the role of the Blue Berets, he declares, 'If the United States allows that claim to go unchallenged, its discretion in using force to advance its national interests is likely to be inhibited in the future.'[16] Or again, on the subject of the gigantic sums owed to the United Nations by America: 'Many Republicans in Congress – and perhaps a majority – not only do not care about losing the General Assembly vote but actually see it as a "make my day" outcome. Indeed, once the vote is lost . . . this will simply provide further evidence to why nothing more should be paid to the UN Systems.'[17]

John Bolton has brought in a special adviser, David Wurmser, a friend of Richard Perle, who also collaborated with Benyamin Netanyahu when the latter was Prime Minister. His wife Meyrav is the co-founder of the Middle East Media Research Institute. This organization, whose other founder was Colonel Yigal Carmon, a former officer in Israeli military intelligence, translates the most hard-hitting articles in the Arab press and exposes the dreadful – and unfortunately all too real – anti-semitism that so powerfully affects this region.

But the same organization also translates other articles, which seem to espouse the overall pattern of American policies in the Middle East. On the first page of their Internet site, on 24 April 2003, a few days after Syria had started to make an appearance in the speeches of Donald Rumsfeld, you could find a Kuwaiti article explaining that the regime of Bachir el-Assad was 'more criminal than Saddam's'.[18] This translation is tendentious - it represents Arab opinion as aligned on Washington policies, which is totally false: almost no political leader in the Middle East – not to mention the man in the street – would support a military intervention in Syria, the repercussions of which would be completely unpredictable.

And yet Syria seems well and truly to figure on the hawks' second black-list, drawn up by Douglas Feith at the end of 2002. However, Afghanistan apart, the war in Iraq and the overthrow of Saddam Hussein have long been one of the hawks' main objectives. Just like the weakening of Syria.

7

The Middle East in Focus

The same David Wurmser I mentioned in the last chapter was the author, with Richard Perle and Douglas Feith, of an ultra-confidential report called 'Clean Break', delivered to the Israeli Prime Minister Netanyahu in 1996, that encompassed two main objectives, both developed with Israel's interests in mind: dismembering Iraq, and neutralizing Syria. In it, you could for instance read the following:

> Jordan has challenged Syria's regional ambitions recently by suggesting the restoration of the Hashemites in Iraq. Since Iraq's future could affect the strategic balance in the Middle East profoundly, it would be understandable that Israel has an interest in supporting the Hashemites in their efforts to redefine Iraq, including such measures as: visiting Jordan as the first official state visit, even before a visit to the United States, of the new Netanyahu government; supporting King Hussein by providing him with some tangible security measures to protect his regime against Syrian subversion; encouraging – through influence in the U.S. business community – investment in Jordan to shift structurally Jordan's economy away from dependence on Iraq; and diverting Syria's attention by using Lebanese opposition elements to destabilize Syrian control of Lebanon. . . . Israel can shape its strategic environment, in cooperation with Turkey and Jordan, by weakening, containing, and even rolling back Syria. This effort can focus on removing Saddam Hussein from power in Iraq – an important Israeli strategic objective in its own right – as a means of foiling Syria's regional ambitions. One way to do it: securing tribal alliances with Arab tribes that cross into Syrian territory and are hostile to the Syrian ruling elite.[1]

Apart from this geostrategic advice, which bears a strange resemblance to an 'instructions manual' for the current war, Perle and his colleagues go further. They declare: 'Given the nature of the regime in Damascus, it is both natural and moral that Israel abandon the slogan "comprehensive peace" and move to contain Syria, drawing attention to its weapons of mass destruction program, and rejecting "land for peace" deals on the Golan Heights.'[2]

This document even contained 'advice' on communication strategies that could attract the sympathy and attention of the Americans when Benyamin Netanyahu visited their country. The new Prime Minister should, for example, formulate his political objectives in a language familiar to the Americans, using terms which had captured the attention of successive administrations during the Cold War.

He was advised to propose an extended cooperation in the area of anti-ballistic defence treaties, as that 'would broaden Israel's base of support among many in the United States Congress who may know little about Israel, but care very much about missile defense'.[3] Again in the words of this document, the adoption of such positions could contribute to the future decision to move the American Embassy from Tel Aviv to Jerusalem, a subject of great interest to many members of Congress, 'including those who know very little about Israel'.[4]

So the war on Iraq is not a new decision for the hawks in this administration. It is not the result of that 'inquiry', which never satisfied anyone, and which was supposed to enable the links between Al Qaeda and Saddam Hussein to be established irrefutably. The war, in fact, constitutes the realization in concrete form of older strategies designed to reshape the balance of power that prevails today in the Middle East.

But a reading of this report leaves one question open: what is the real objective of this operation? Is it the pursuit of American interests, or the reinforcement of Israeli's position in this region, something to be brought about in concert with Likud? Even if this is the case, this 'Clean Break' policy is very far from meeting with unanimous agreement in Israel. Even a great number of those who voted for Likud at the last elections hope one day to see a rebirth of the peace process, in one form or another. However,

Richard Perle explains (again in 'Clean Break') that this same peace process 'undermines the legitimacy of the nation and leads Israel into strategic paralysis'.[5]

'The Global Leadership of the United States'

Whatever may be the main cause – Israeli or American – that the hawks are trying to defend, to consider the dismemberment of a nation as complex as Iraq, which would then be joined to a kingdom as unstable as Jordan, like the pieces of a banal jigsaw puzzle, reveals the degree of over-confidence and lack of realism endemic in the thinking and planning of these men. But the document delivered to Netanyahu, which detailed Israeli interests and the means of defending them, via the overthrow of the Iraqi regime and the weakening of Syria, was complemented four years later by a version that was drawn up for Americans, and in particular for George W. Bush. There were two main differences between this and the original document. First and foremost, in formulation. The latter uses a terminology more familiar to the Americans, rather as if its authors (more or less the same as before) had drawn inspiration from the advice they themselves had showered on Netanyahu. The second difference resides in the fact that this document does not mention any dismemberment of Iraq, even if this idea resurfaced a few months ago in remarks made by Wolfowitz. This second, 'watered-down' version is tailor-made to please its readers, to get its general message across, and to avoid getting bogged down in over-precise considerations. This report was drawn up under the aegis of another Washington think tank, the Project for the New American Century (PNAC), aimed at promoting the 'global leadership of the United States'. PNAC brings together pro-Israeli hawks, Likud sympathizers, and members of the Christian extreme Right in America. On its internet site, PNAC details the links between Arafat and terrorism, drawing on the documentation of the Israeli Army! You have to admit that there are more objective sources around.

The PNAC report, written for future leaders of the Bush administration in September 2000, was entitled 'Rebuilding America's

Defenses: Strategies, Forces and Resources for a New Century'. In it we learn, for example, what the failed attempts to establish a link between Saddam Hussein and Osama bin Laden might have allowed one to foresee many months previously. The war on terrorism was merely a pretext to invade Iraq. The report declares: 'The United States has for decades sought to play a more permanent role in Gulf regional security. While the unresolved conflict with Iraq provides the immediate justification, the need for a substantial American force present in the Gulf transcends the issue of the regime of Saddam Hussein.'[6]

As for the armed forces of the United States, the report describes them as 'the cavalry on the new American frontier'.[7] It is impossible not to recall the advice lavished by these same men on Netanyahu: use a language familiar to Americans if you want to convince them. Here, such remarks combine stereotypes (cavalry, new frontier) and constitute a fine example of successful communication. Especially if judged by the invasion of Iraq that followed.

The hawks had already tried repeatedly to impose their point of view at the highest level of the executive. Some time after the fall of the Berlin Wall, under the first Bush administration, a decisive conversation between Dick Cheney and Paul Wolfowitz spelled the first victory for the neo-conservatives. Cheney, the then Defense Secretary, had set up a think tank including in particular Paul Wolfowitz and Lewis Libby, another supporter of the Iraq war. The objective assigned to these men was considerable: they were to define the main lines of a new American foreign policy in the post-Cold War world. Colin Powell, then Chief of Staff of the combined forces, was invited to draw up a rival report setting out a vision of the world and of international relations that would be more moderate than that of the hawks.

Cheney settled on a date: 21 May 1990. Wolfowitz's and Powell's groups respectively would each have one hour to set out their recommendations. Cheney would then report to the President, who would deliver an address of the highest importance on the new American foreign policy.

When the fateful day arrived, Wolfowitz spoke first. In his view, America should shape the rest of the world, and no longer remain content with reacting to events that had already happened. In this way, she would be able to foresee the emergence of rival powers and establish her supremacy.

Wolfowitz considerably overran the hour allocated to Colin Powell for his presentation, but Dick Cheney let him go on and develop his fundamental idea, the one that, twelve years later, would be used to justify the overthrow of Saddam Hussein: America can no longer wait to be attacked before responding. It is its duty to intervene where, when, and how it desires. It should shape events so as not to have to submit to them.

Colin Powell had to leave without having made his presentation. The Defense Secretary courteously arranged another meeting, a fortnight later. But the briefing that Cheney gave George Bush Sr bore the clear imprint of Wolfowitz's ideas. Powell had already lost.

The head of the American executive was ready to give a speech that would have gone down in history, since it constituted a veritable turning-point in the development of this traditionally introverted nation that hates looking outwards and getting mixed up with the world's problems. But Bush's address, programmed for the very time the Iraqi tanks were pushing into Kuwait, was cancelled.

Throughout the 1990s the vision of the hawks seemed to become increasingly sharp, like the radar of a fighter plane scanning a deserted horizon until it finally 'picks up' a target and shoots off towards it. Their global foreign policy doctrine, based on being able to anticipate threats and reduce rival powers, applicable to any region and any circumstances, finally fixed on a more precise objective: the Middle East, the source of perpetual instability and the theatre of interests that go beyond mere regional conflicts.

The at times very close links between the hawks and Israel (where Wolfowitz's sister lives), as well as the identity of outlook between these men and the leaders of Likud, have forged in them a sense of absolute certainty. The interests of America and Israel are bound together. These two democracies must support each other, whatever the costs, to face the Arab world which has replaced the Soviet Union in the role of adversary. An adversary that must, if necessary, be freed by force.

'The Arabs Incapable of Democracy'

The remarks of Bernard Lewis, a famous orientalist close to the neo-conservatives, are edifying. According to Paul Wolfowitz, he has 'brilliantly placed the relationships and the issues of the Middle East into their larger context, with truly objective, original – and always independent – thought. Bernard has taught [us] how to understand the complex and important history of the Middle East and use it to guide us where we will go next to build a better world for generations.'[8]

This same 'orientalist', speaking to the American Enterprise Institute (of which Perle is a member, as well as Douglas Feith and the wife of Vice-President Cheney), spoke of two possible points of view about establishing a truly democratic post-Saddam regime.

> The first could be summed up like this: The Arabs are incapable of democratic government. Arabs are different from us, and we must be more, shall we say, reasonable both in what we expect from them and in what they may expect from us. Whatever we do, these countries will be ruled by corrupt tyrants. The aim of foreign policy, therefore, should be to make sure that they are friendly tyrants rather than hostile.
>
> The other point of view is somewhat different. It begins more or less from the same position – that Arab countries are not democracies and that establishing democracies within Arab societies will be difficult. Yet, Arabs are teachable and democratic governance ought to be possible for them, provided we proctor and gradually launch them on our way, or I should say on their way.
>
> That point of view is known as imperialism. It was the method adopted in the British and French empires, in their mandated territories and in some of their colonies, creating governments in their own image. In Iraq, in Syria, and elsewhere, the British created constitutional monarchies and the French created unstable republics. None of them worked very well. But hope still remains.[9]

So: are Arabs 'incapable of democratic government', or might they be 'teachable'? These alarming comments do not come from a marginalized man, whose extremist views are restricted to a small audience. Richard Perle spoke several times at the same conference. Paul Wolfowitz, as we have already seen, could not praise Bernard Lewis – a world-renowned expert, who during the Second World War worked for the British intelligence services – too highly. And yet, at this time, the American President was preparing to wage war on Iraq and giving his assurance that everything had been done to avoid 'the clash of civilizations', a formula invented by none other than Lewis, before being taken up by Samuel Huntington.

Already, under the Clinton administration, Baghdad constituted a prime target for the hawks. In 1998 the PNAC published an open letter to the President, asking him to engage in unilateral military action, without passing through the Security Council of the United States. The letter, which was signed by Richard Perle, but also by Donald Rumsfeld and Paul Wolfowitz, declared that 'in any case, American policy cannot continue to be crippled by a misguided insistence on unanimity in the UN Security Council'.[10]

A few weeks later another think tank, the Committee for Peace and Security in the Gulf (CPSG), asked Bill Clinton this time to recognize a provisional Iraqi government, under the leadership of members of the Iraq National Council (INC), and bringing together exiled dissidents. This recognition would have constituted, in the words of the CPSG, the first step of a 'comprehensive political and military strategy for bringing down Saddam and his regime'.[11] The INC should launch attacks from the 'liberated zones' in which a no-fly ban had been imposed on Iraqi planes, while American aviation destroyed the military infrastructures. The plan proposed to Bill Clinton also asked for the deployment of American troops in the surrounding countries, just in case things started to go wrong.

In addition to Perle, who jointly presided over the CPSG, this second letter was signed by Rumsfeld, Wolfowitz, Feith, Abrams, and Bolton. This strategy of creating more and more committees, organizations and other think tanks is well known in Washington. As one member of the State Department explained to me:

Perle and the rest of the hawks have used this method for a long time. It gives the impression to public opinion, and to certain members of Congress, that the neo-conservative wave is being transformed into a veritable flood tide. One centre starts lobbying to attack Iraq, the following day so does another one, and the following week your favourite newspaper published a letter on the first page coming from yet a third 'research institute'. They all speak with one voice. That impresses people. You think that the majority is coming over to their opinions. But it's completely false. In reality, it's the same men who constantly reappear in a different costume. They are few in number, but very well organized and very effective: inflexible ideologues, as well as being real professionals when it comes to communication.[12]

For the Good of Israel?

When you think about the dossier compiled by PNAC for the current administration, the letters addressed to Bill Clinton, and, on the other side, the 'advice' showered on Benyamin Netanyahu, you can only wonder: are the hawks using the Israeli dossier to promote their own ideas of American greatness, which must at all costs be restored? Or are they using their current positions to support the policies of the Israeli Right, under the leadership of Ariel Sharon?

A former Israeli politician, close to Yitzhak Rabin, and opposed to the policies of the hawks, declares:

They think they can restore American greatness. But at the same time this increased power will serve, in their view, Israel's interests. Because they are theorists. For them, the balance of forces in the region can be defined by numbers and on maps. For them, it's mathematics: bring down Saddam, weaken Syria, and that way you'll bring the Palestinians to their knees.[13]

But an opinion such as this is far from prevailing in the cabinet of the current Prime Minister, who considers that operation 'Iraqi Freedom' is a real piece of luck for the State of Israel. Exactly like the hawks, Ariel Sharon considers that an Iraq that has been rid of Saddam Hussein will be able to become a valid discussion partner in peace negotiations in the Middle East. Furthermore, the weakening of Syria would sideline Israel's sworn enemy. Damascus, after all, harbours almost all of the terrorist movements that bring bloodshed to Israeli towns, including Hamas, Islamic Jihad and Hezbollah.

Everything that gets decided in Washington on the subject of the Middle East, under the influence of the hawks, is in line with the policies advocated by Ariel Sharon. And yet it is difficult to understand how the arrival of the Americans – a power that as everyone knows tends to look after Israel – in Baghdad could calm the ferment among the Palestinian people, whose demands are far from concerning Baghdad. Whatever government emerges in Iraq, even if it is fiercely pro-Western, the population will never accept seeing its leaders negotiating with Ariel Sharon. You cannot gauge the degree of absolute rage that surrounds this personage through-out the Arab world. And the thinking of the hawks – shared by Likud – which consists of settling the problems of the Middle East over the head of its populations risks showing its limitations pretty soon. To embark on peace negotiations with the current Israeli government would constitute real political suicide for future Iraqi political leaders. Washington seems not to understand this.

Not content with conducting its regional politics in accordance with the wishes of the Israeli Right, America has taken to launch-ing outspoken attacks on Ariel Sharon's sworn enemy, Yasser Arafat. Senator Joseph Liebermann, during a visit from Benyamin Netanyahu to the American Senate on 10 April 2002, echoed a point of view that is widely prevalent in Washington: 'the suicide killers in Israel', said Liebermann, 'are out of the same cloth as the suicide killers who killed 3,000 Americans on September 11th.' President Yasser Arafat 'had hijacked the legitimate Palestinian cause'. And he added that 'no one was better suited to speak at this moment than his friend, Benyamin Netanyahu', who repre-sents the hardliners in Likud.[14]

It is interesting to observe that Netanyahu is again following the advice of Richard Perle and Douglas Feith in the 'Clean Break' dossier, since his speech does not focus on Israeli problems: he lumps them together with 11 September so that his American audience will feel 'involved'. However, Al Qaeda has not yet com-

mitted any act of terrorism on Israeli soil, and Palestinian terrorist movements have never been active in the United States. But
this undeniable fact does not prevent him from declaring, 'If we
do not shut down the terror factories that Arafat is hosting – those
terror factories that are producing human bombs – it is only a
matter of time before suicide bombers will terrorize your cities
here in America.'[15]

This blackmail on terror is particularly effective in an America
still shocked by 11 September. Above all, it allows people
to justify, in an Israeli context, the application of the doctrine
of 'preventive war' adopted by the hawks in Afghanistan and in
Iraq.

'Bibi' Netanyahu, the same day, also went to the American
Enterprise Institute, the rallying point of the neo-conservatives. In
his address he explained that 'Arafat's regime has to be eliminated,
along with those of his supporters, especially Iraq. Nothing less
will stop terrorism, so let's just do it.'[16]

'A Resolutely Unintellectual President'

As can be seen, American policy in the Middle East is in complete
harmony with the aspirations of Likud. Is this a coincidence, or a
desire on Washington's part to serve the interests defended by the
Israeli Right?

It is difficult to say. But what can be stated is that the hawks
see Likud policies as the only ones able to restore stability to Israel
and, thereby, to the whole region. Ariel Sharon is applying to the
State of Israel the remedy that Richard Perle and his acolytes are
trying to apply to the Middle East as a whole: overthrow existing
structures from top to bottom, so as to create a seedbed more
favourable to their interests.

Uri Avnery, the founder of Gush Shalom, an organization that
militates in favour of dialogue between Israelis and Palestinians,
declared on the subject of the hawks and their policies:

> the style sounds vaguely familiar. In the early 80s, I heard about
> several plans like this from Ariel Sharon (which I published at

the time). His head was full of grand designs for restructuring the Middle East, the creation of an Israeli security zone from Pakistan to Central Africa, the overthrow of regimes and installing others in their stead, moving a whole people (the Palestinians) and so forth.

I can't help it, but the winds blowing now in Washington remind me of Sharon. I have absolutely no proof that the Bushes got their ideas from him, even if all of them seem to have been mesmerized by him. But the style is the same – a mixture of megalomania, creativity, arrogance, ignorance and superficiality. An explosive mixture.

Sharon's grand design floundered, as we know. The bold flights of imagination and the superficial logic did not help – Sharon simply did not understand the real currents of history. I fear that the band of Bush, Cheney, Rumsfield, Rice, Wolfowitz, Perle and all the other little Sharons are suffering from the same syndrome.[17]

But the support of the Israeli government is total, and even public. In August 2002 the Israeli Deputy Defence Minister declared on the subject of Iraq: 'If the Americans do not do this now, it will be harder to do it in the future. In a year or two, Saddam Hussein will be further along in developing weapons of mass destruction. It is a world interest, but especially an American interest to attack Iraq. And as Deputy Defence Minister, I can tell you that the United States will receive any assistance from Israel'.[18]

But for the time being it is rather Israel which is receiving total assistance from the United States in its pursuit of a new regional order. Wolfowitz, who is considered to be one of the main architects of the war on Iraq, has gained a surprising influence with the President, especially in view of the position he occupies (he is only no. 2 in the Pentagon). The man the President calls 'Wolfie' has become a close conversation partner of George W. Bush. The *New York Times Magazine* declares:

Wolfowitz's moralistic streak and the generally sunny view of the world's possibilities may explain the affinity between the born-again and resolutely unintellectual president and this man he calls 'Wolfie' . . . A senior official who has watched the two men interact says that Wolfowitz and the President have reinforced each other in their faith in 'a strategic transformation of the whole region'.[19]

In the surprising collusion of interests between Israel and America, there are some rather disturbing facts. Certain highly placed officials, even within the Bush administration, are asking themselves about Israel's direct role in the way the United States embarked on war. The FBI has recently announced, for instance, that it was exploring the possibility that a foreign government is manipulating to increase the support for a military campaign against Iraq. In fact, everyone remembers the 'irrefutable proofs' that America tirelessly promised to provide of the manufacture of weapons of mass destruction – proofs which convinced no one, so slender and controversial were they.

'Clearly, it's Israel they're talking about,' an official in Mossad told me.

> But as far as I'm aware, there was never any operation aimed at leading the United States into error, manipulating the Americans so they'd start this war. The risks would be too significant for us, if the public ever got wind of it one day. The documents that Colin Powell showed the United Nations don't come from Israel. But there is cooperation between the secret services of the two countries. And, with the current government, the information transmitted to American intelligence was certainly meant to emphasize the idea of an immediate danger. To put it more clearly, the information was correct, but certainly 'selected' at source. Likud did nothing to calm things down and hold the Americans back. It wasn't in its interest.[20]

The interests of Israel, or rather of the 'hardliners' like Sharon and Netanyahu, seem to be the first criterion to be taken into acccount by Israel. What strikes an observer right now is the fact that the history of this conflict was written seven years earlier.

The overthrow of Saddam Hussein has taken place. And now, what is to be done with Iraq? Or rather, how could Israel – in the view of Likud and the hawks – benefit from this new situation? In 1996 the men who are today sitting in the Pentagon thought they could attach Iraq to Jordan. But in October 2002 the Strategic Group for Analysis and Forecast, STRATFOR, revealed that Dick Cheney was thinking of two options concerning Iraq: integrating it into neighbouring Jordan (as in 'Clean Break') or dismembering it into three states: one autonomous, the other attached (again) to Jordan, and the third, the Shiite zone, integrated into Kuwait.

It is extremely difficult to follow American logic. Apart from Israel, in whose interest can it be that the enormous country of Iraq be *de facto* attached to the only country 'friendly' to Israel in the region?

A significant majority of Iraq is Shiite – 60 per cent. Relations between Shiites and Sunnis are rarely cordial. But Jordan and Kuwait are almost exclusively Sunni. How could one hope such a graft to take? And above all, why bother? Setting up a stable democratic regime within Iraq will be quite difficult enough as it is.

Furthermore, the Americans intervened in the Gulf in 1991 after Saddam had invaded Kuwait on the – justifiable – pretext that this micro-state had always been part of Iraq. The international community was unanimous in its condemnation. Today Washington would like to attach Iraq to its neighbours – something which is just as lacking in legitimacy.

'There's a lot of talk about these plans in Washington,' says one expert. 'Cut Iraq into pieces . . . But frankly, the general feeling can be summed up like this: "They'll back down". Very few people think the hawks would go that far. It would be one step too far.'[21]

This is altogether probable. It must not be forgotten that the men who drew up 'Clean Break' are theorists, who conceive of politics from a totally abstract point of view, one that is often cut off from realities on the ground. In compiling the dossier destined for Netanyahu, they were getting their ideas down on paper, destined for a nation they did not govern. Today they are in key posts in the most powerful country in the world, and reality has caught up with them.

But the mere fact of thinking such thoughts shows the extent to which the interests of Israel (at least as they envisage them) are dear to them. And it matters little to them if this entails huge risks for that country.

Washington Attacks the Wrong Targets

These risks are far from being a thing of the past for Israel: a British official told *Newsweek*, in August 2002, 'Everyone wants to go to Baghdad. Real men want to go to Teheran.'[22] The big Israeli daily, *Ha'aretz*, declared in February 2003 that John Bolton had claimed to an Israeli official that, once they had finished with Iraq, the United States would take care of Iran, Syria, and North Korea.

Things will get seriously complicated for Israel when the Americans turn their attentions to Damascus. For if the conflict that brought America into opposition with Saddam Hussein had never been really settled, so that George W. Bush had a ready-made pretext (he has also stated, 'After all, this is the guy who tried to kill my dad' – an allusion to the failed attempt of 1993),[23] attacking Syria will be much more difficult to justify. If the GIs are sent into that country, it will appear more and more clear that America is waging the neighbourhood war that Israel cannot allow itself. For the link between Al Qaeda and Syria is (very!) far from being established. You can, of course, hear Donald Rumsfeld coming out with the old refrain about weapons of mass destruction, but nobody is fooled any more.

Syria is on America's black-list since the hawks have so decided. Here too, people are asking questions. There are several countries in which Osama bin Laden's organization is firmly implanted: Somalia is a veritable safe haven for Al Qaeda, and no intelligence agency in the world will deny as much. But it is Syria that they're going to attack. Damascus shelters terrorists just as dangerous as those of Al Qaeda, but their actions are focused on Israel. Hence any American military operation in this country will be seen as gross manipulation, aimed at eliminating adversaries that Likud cannot attack head-on.

If it was hard to understand the real reasons for a war in Iraq after 11 September, the threats hanging over Syria complicate things even more. To put it more clearly, Washington is attacking the wrong targets – regimes that are not in the least likeable, but which are for all that not in the least implicated in the terrible attacks committed in 1991. Despite the rain of fire and the extent of the retaliation, the dead of the World Trade Center, the Pentagon, and the Pennsylvania plane are still unavenged.

After Afghanistan, Somalia, Yemen and Sudan would certainly have constituted more adequate targets, if the hawks really were attacking Al Qaeda.

The benefits the Israeli Right expected as a result of this (or these) conflict(s) is a subject that the hawks and their allies try to keep within the bounds of the greatest discretion. At the end of 2002 the *New York Times* unveiled the existence of a revealing document advising Israeli leaders and American Jews to keep a low profile on the subject of the Iraqi campaign:

> If your goal is regime change, you must be much more careful with your language because of the potential backlash. You do not want Americans to believe that the war on Iraq is being waged to protect Israel rather than to protect America. . . . Let American politicians fight it out on the floor of Congress and the media. Let the nations of the world argue in front of the UN. Your silence allows everyone to focus on Iraq rather than Israel.[24]

All too clearly, it is by keeping a low profile that you evade the embarrassing question: who profits from the war? Not Israel, in any case, which risks bearing the brunt of the experience. But, rather, the supporters of force, in Washington and Tel Aviv. Two groups:

(1) In Israel, hardliners in Likud, who are considered by some as the heroes of the numerous wars which Israel has had to face, convinced as they are that terrorism must be eradicated together with all those who support it. Convinced too that negotiation will not defuse the tensions, or only after a clear and decisive show of Israeli force.

(2) In Washington, ideologues who have never touched a weapon in their whole lives, who have never experienced war, but who handle it like a particularly alluring intellectual concept. They are the most influential of the men around President Bush. They have enormous power at their disposal. They are convinced that they are working for the good of Israel: the war they are waging

in the name of America, perhaps sincerely, completely serves the views of their counterparts, the Israeli hawks. And it is precisely for that reason that this war is seriously endangering the future of the State of Israel.

This situation opens the gates to every unpredictable twist and every interpretation, whatever the result of the battles fought. If America and its strike force are perceived as appendages of the Israeli Right in the region, the dreams of democracy and progress in the Middle East will soon be buried. Even worse, the situation could rapidly become uncontrollable. And, under pressure from public opinion at home, the Americans would quite simply clear out, as they did in Vietnam or Somalia. But the Israelis are condemned to stay put.

8

The New Jerusalem?

A supplementary proof that the policy of the hawks is not conducted in Israel's overall interest but in the interest of Likud lies in the fact that this party uses the networks of the neoconservatives and the Christian extreme Right in America to finance its electoral campaigns. On 8 January 2001 a gathering of over 250,000 people was organized by the One Jerusalem Foundation, which militates on behalf of the recognition of this city as the indivisible capital of Israel. Speaker after speaker lambasted the peace initiatives of Ehud Barak. Among the speakers was Ehud Olmert, mayor of the city and a very influential member of Likud, who has since become Vice Prime Minister and Minister of Industry and Trade. At his side was Ronald Lauder, the heir of Estée Lauder, the then head of the confederation of presidents of Jewish associations, and also a fierce supporter of Likud and Ariel Sharon.

One month away from the elections that were to bring the latter to power, the speeches took on the appearance of a veritable electoral campaign in favour if the Right. Ronald Lauder, on his return to the United States, was sharply criticized by his peers – the same ones he was representing during this whole event – for his partisan, militant attitude.

The very next day, the *Jerusalem Post* declared that 'the State Controller Eliezer Goldberg was monitoring the rally', since One Jerusalem presents itself as a charitable organization.[1] For this reason it is forbidden to support a party or a candidate at election time. But the outspoken criticisms of the Labour Party, the ideas advocated by the speakers, as well as the fact that they belonged to or were close to Likud, created a situation that was, to say the least, paradoxical: an apolitical organization acclaiming Sharon's positions and castigating Barak's did not exactly seem very neutral, especially one month before the elections.

And who do we find among the founders of this organization? Douglas Feith, today Under-Secretary of Defense for Policy in the Bush administration. At his side, the director of One Jerusalem is a man on whom we need to linger for a few moments, if we are to understand to which school of thought the current no. 3 of the Pentagon seems to subscribe. Yechiel Leiter was the author of a polemic on the Oslo agreements – which gave some hope for a pacific solution to the conflict – entitled *A Peace to Resist*. In addition, in May 1994, he published an extremely pernicious article in the *Jerusalem Post*, referring to the risks of assassination to which Rabin would be exposed if he pursued his quest for peace: 'The government is sending the message that no number of Jewish lives is too great to sacrifice for the implementation of its political programme – one that is supported by no more than half the people . . . But rational argument will not be enough to prevent the first Israeli assassination on Israeli soil.' Leiter also wonders, in the same article: 'Is political assassination a possibility in Israel today? One desperately wishes the answer were no. Yet the possibility of a depraved attempt by Jewish extremists is one we can no longer afford to ignore.'[2]

An Inextricable Network

While he did not endorse such an eventuality, he nonetheless referred to it as a growing danger, 'as long as the government insists on its divisive course'. A form of indirect blackmail which, without implying as much, all the same threatens those working for peace. We know what happened shortly afterwards to its fiercest defender, Yitzhak Rabin.

Douglas Feith is one of the founders of the organization today led by Yechiel Leiter. It is merely one of the links in an inextricable network of 'charitable' foundations, linking up the Israeli extreme Right and its American supporters. New Jerusalem is an even more striking example: founded in 1998 by Mayor Ehud Olmert so as to raise funds for the city, this foundation generates colossal sums destined for various different projects, each of them more difficult to verify than the others. The municipal councillor Anat Hoffman, a member of the centre-left Meretz Party, explains that there is 'no accountability here'.[3]

In spring 2002 Olmert went to Texas, where he received more than 400,000 dollars for his foundation from the Christian extreme Right, who are convinced (as I have already explained) that Israel belongs only to the Jewish people, and in particular that their complete resettlement on this land constitutes the indispensable precondition for the advent of the end of the world.

Olmert is one of the pivots of these 'donations' from extremist Christians. 'He goes to the United States more often than any other official from this country', an Israeli journalist told me. And the sums he manages to raise are considerable. For example, on 15 October 2002 Olmert took part in another 'prayer summit for Jerusalem' in San Diego, at a thousand dollars a place, which brought him in almost half a million dollars for the evening. Four days earlier, in Washington, a dinner of 'Christian solidarity with Israel' was held in the company of the Texan senator Tom DeLay, also in aid of the 'charitable' organizations of the Mayor of Jerusalem.

New Jerusalem was for long a phantom foundation, without the slightest legal existence in Israel. This allowed funds from the United States to be allocated more flexibly. To such an extent, indeed, that the *Jerusalem Post*, on 9 April 2000, reported that opposition members on the Jerusalem City Council feared that the Mayor had not registered the activities of his foundation since he would have used it to raise funds for his own political needs.[4]

While Ehud Olmert's foundation was still in limbo, and was to remain so for a long time, it was granted the status of a charitable organization in the United States, which exempted it from all tax! And this is despite the fact that it has not the slightest physical existence in the country, apart from its American representative, Garry Wallin, who is also treasurer of the American Israeli Public Affairs Committee (AIPAC – the 'official' pro-Israeli lobbying organization in the United States) and president of the Gush Etzion Foundation, in homage to the first colonies implanted in this Palestinian region after the 1967 war.

This man ensures the money gets through to Israel, where it is placed in the care of Raviv and Uri Messer, the 'juridical' advisers of Ehud Olmert. According to this same Raviv, the New Jerusalem Foundation works with the rabbi Yechiel Eckstein, from the International Fellowship of Christians and Jews, an organization based in Chicago and Jerusalem.[5]

Although this cannot be verified, Eckstein has declared to the press that he had obtained over 30 million dollars in gifts, principally in America, since 1993.[6] Esther Levin, the president of a 'rival' association (the National Unity Coalition for Israel), claims that Eckstein repatriates more than 30 million dollars *per year*, and that this money then heads to unknown destinations where it is swallowed up.

Be this is it may, the rabbi was appointed by Ariel Sharon as public relations ambassador to the international Christian community. His various links represent a priceless capital insofar as the donations of ultra-religious American Christians never cease to grow. Since their ideas naturally incline them towards Likud, rather than towards the Labour Party and other members in the peace camp, the foundations and prayer dinners of the Mayor of Jerusalem have a fine future ahead of them.

In the official documents drawn up for the American tax office, we find that One Jerusalem (founded by Douglas Feith) has its headquarters at 136 East 39th Street, in Manhattan. Now this ordinary and discreet apartment block is also the home of One Israel and B'Nai Zion. The former is a charitable foundation, but exclusively meant for colonists in the Palestinian territories. There you are given amazing explanations of how donations are used to buy night sight systems or armoured vehicles for the 'pioneers' in Hebron, Gaza and elsewhere.

The latter, B'Nai Zion, is one of the oldest and most radical Jewish organizations in America. Founded in 1908, it became, from the 1920s onwards, the shop window of the movement of Vladimir Jobotinsky, the father of the 'revisionist Zionists', and the intellectual guru of Menachem Begin, with particularly radical ideas. He wrote, for example, that there was no disagreement between Jews and Arabs – just a natural conflict. There would be no agreement possible with Palestinian Arabs, who would never accept Zionism until they saw that they were up against an 'iron wall' and were forced to realize that the Jewish presence would be permanent.

B'Nai Zion finances the ultra-radical Jewish colonies on the West Bank. One of its most influential members, Milton Shapiro, is also the national treasurer of the Friends of Likud in America.

According to an investigation in the *Executive Intelligence Review*, Omri Sharon, Ariel Sharon's son, is allegedly suspected of having used one of the branches of B'Nai Zion to finance his father's campaign.[7] The American Red Magen David Adom, an Israeli Red Cross organization that is, however, not recognized by the International Committee since it works *within* the army during its operations in the Palestinian territories, was founded by B'Nai Zion and, again according to the *Executive Intelligence Review*, is allegedly used to repatriate foreign money via a Cypriot bank.

In 2001, in the United States, societies serving as fronts would thus have allowed funds to be transferred to Likud via Ariel Sharon's campaign adviser, Art Finkelstein. Another name is mentioned in this amorphous group: that of Ariel Genger, a personal friend of Ariel Sharon and a secret emissary of the latter to the White House, with access to high places in the Bush administration. This once prosperous businessman placed his two chemical plants into receivership to escape debts of 224 million dollars. He is, however, still a member of an investment fund, the Challenge Fund, which very generously finances Israeli hi-tech firms.

In the 1980s, at the time of Irangate, certain of these same networks 'accidentally' benefited from a transfer of funds from the Sultan of Brunei, who gave 10 million dollars to Washington to secretly arm the Nicaragua Contras – just after meeting an American official in London. This mysterious emissary, who had travelled to London under an assumed identity, was in fact none other than Elliott Abrams: the current White House hawk, a friend of Feith, Perle and Wolfowitz.

The 'Murawiec Report'

The way the hawks talk of the greatness of America that needs to be restored, of the war on terrorism and weapons of mass destruction, is seriously put in question by their former views. When, in

1996, they explained to Benyamin Netanyahu what were the regional security policies that could ensure the stability of Israel, they presented him with a very complete – too complete! – guide to current American strategy, giving the impression today that 11 September and the 'hunt' for Osama bin Laden are merely a useful pretext for them to put into application what they have been dreaming of for years. After the tragedies in New York, Washington and Pennsylvania, their concept of 'preventive war' has become the refrain of President Bush. But this 1996 document, destined for Israel, shows that the United States is not the only preoccupation of the hawks.

Their political honesty can be doubted insofar as these two objectives – consisting of simultaneously promoting American and Israeli interests – risk turning out to be totally incompatible. For Washington, which is deemed to be leading a war of liberation in the Arab world, an unconditional support for the Israeli Right, and even – for certain parties that have come together around Ariel Sharon – the extreme Right, represents the worst possible option if they want to win the sympathy of the peoples and leaders of that region. The hawks know as much. But they nonetheless continue to apply the different stages of 'Clean Break', justifying it by a supposed war on terror which it is getting harder and harder to believe in.

Indeed, they are not linked to Israel, but to the most outspoken organizations, the ones most opposed to peace. George W. Bush cannot or will not see this. Or else he doesn't give a damn. But the three possibilities entail the same consequences: a gradual and inevitable stiffening of opinion in the Muslim world in the face of a foreign power which insists at all costs on seeing through its objectives in the region. With those who are already being called by many people 'Sharon's men' at the top of the Pentagon, the situation can only get worse.

In summer 2002 the Defense Policy Board, which Richard Perle was then chairing, organized a briefing which was to say the least surprising, in which a man called Laurent Murawiec, a researcher with Rand Corporation, urged the administration to declare Saudi Arabia an enemy of the United States, and 'to give it an ultimatum to stop backing terrorism or face seizure of its oil fields and its financial assets invested in the United States'.[8]

Saudi Arabia gives no direct support to Al Qaeda. It is the last country that can be suspected of that, insofar as Osama bin Laden has there been sentenced to death *in absentia*, for his openly expressed hatred of the current monarchy – a hatred that is reciprocated by the different princes of the royal family, for whom he represents a sworn enemy. But apart from that, it is true that Arabia supports – Hezbollah excepted – all the terrorist movements on the rampage in Israel, and that this country is probably one of the most vicious in its anti-semitism and its racial hatred for the Jewish people. In the numerous telethons organized on the national channel in favour of the Palestinian people, it has been possible to hear, for example, one imam declaring: 'Respect nothing of the Jews – neither their religion, nor their soul, nor their flesh. Take Jewish women since they were made for you, and reduce them to slavery!'

The political and social system of this country has, however, never prevented the United States from considering it as a permanent ally in the region. Even if the religious fundamentalism of this monarchy explains why the air pirates were in the main Saudis, it is totally baseless to believe that the royal family could have endorsed the activities of Al Qaeda. To put it more clearly, its government does not support the terrorism of which America was victim. However, Laurent Murawiec is suggesting that their oil be seized and their assets in the United States frozen – an indirect means of guaranteeing that they will be reduced to poverty.

Who would benefit from such a situation? If Saudi Arabia were led by a 'docile' government, and if the financial manna of oil ceased to flow into the coffers of Hamas or Islamic Jihad, the odds are that Palestinian resistance would be severely diminished.

Once again, the utterances of the hawks seem more destined to smooth the path for the heavy-arm strategies of Likud than to pursue the 11 September terrorists.

Murawiec, the man pushed into the limelight, was of secondary importance, and Perle told *Time* magazine, 'I didn't know what he was going to say, but he had done some serious research on Saudi Arabia.'[9] For the State Department official quoted above, 'Perle knew that he was setting out on a particularly slippery slope in mentioning Saudi Arabia. He wanted to float the idea, but keep an escape route open. Sending Murawiec ahead, without any support, gave him just this opportunity.' And things did indeed turn out badly. The Defense Policy Board briefing provoked a real outcry, a grave crisis between Washington and Riyad, and Rand broke off with Murawiec. And the whole affair was forgotten. But this episode reveals, nonetheless, to what extremes these men are ready to go, when it comes to broadening the current conflict.

9

The New Arms Race

Questions about the loyalty of certain hawks go well beyond their sympathy for Israel. In March 2003 the American journalist Seymour Hersh, of the *New Yorker*, an old stager of investigative journalism, revealed for instance that Richard Perle was one of the associates of the Trireme firm, which invested in particular in 'companies dealing in technology, goods, and services that are of value to homeland security and defense'.[1]

One year later, Trireme had collected 45 million dollars, 20 million of it coming from the aeronautics and military constructor Boeing. But Perle and his associates were still seeking other investors. To help them, they requested aid from one of the most controversial men in the business world, Adnan Khashoggi. This 67-year-old Saudi had previously amassed a considerable fortune as the intermediary of the royal family in arms contracts drawn up with American and European firms. His contacts and his talents as a negotiator had made him a real guarantee of success for an investment fund in search of new capital.

Gerald Hillman, who looks after the direct management of Trireme in the firm's premises in New York, met Khashoggi for the first time in Paris, in the company of a leading Saudi industrialist, potential investor and – above all – native of Iraq.

And it all began with a misunderstanding, one that the Americans were only too happy to foster. The man, Harb Zuhair by name, saw in this affair an opportunity to turn to the American decision-makers so as to put forward his point of view to them, and – even more – to give them the information that he picked up in the course of his various trips to Iraq. Zuhair had access to the highest spheres of Iraqi power, and perhaps to Saddam Hussein himself. He was convinced that a negotiated settlement remained possible: the affair was taking place in December 2002 and this gathering of investors constituted an ideal platform. He told the Trireme officials, 'if we have peace, it would be easy to raise a hundred million. We will bring development to the region.'[2]

As for Trireme and its shareholders, they were after money – why not get it from Saudi Arabia? They did not believe for one second in the value of a political discussion with Zuhair, even if Gerald Hillman was also on the Defense Policy Board, the highly influential Pentagon organization presided over by Perle.

However, they knew that contracts depended on Zuhair's good will, and that a categorical refusal would consign the 100 million dollars promised to oblivion. They had to play the game. And this is exactly what happened.

In the days following the Paris talks, Hillman drew up a twelve-point memorandum, dated 12 December 2002, which stipulated in particular that Saddam Hussein would have to admit that he had 'developed and possesses weapons of mass destruction'.[3] These demands were officially repeated by the Bush administration two months later. The memorandum concluded: 'It's my belief that if the United States obtained the following results it would not go to war against Iraq. He [Saddam Hussein] would then be allowed to resign and leave Iraq immediately with his sons and some of his ministers.'[4]

This memo did not have the slightest official legitimacy. It was not the result of any debate within the administration, and on the diplomatic level Hillman expected nothing from it. It was simply a matter of pulling the wool over the eyes of the Iraqi-Saudi, while hoping that the investments would arrive.

One week later, Hillman sent a second memo: 'Following our recent discussions, we have been thinking about an immediate test to ascertain that Iraq is sincere in its desire to surrender.'[5] Five new conditions were attached to this text. Zuhair described them as absurd, and Khashoggi – an experienced veteran of international negotiations – found them amusing and almost idiotic.

A Schoolgirl Helps to Write these Memos

The amateurish nature of the content can easily be explained: however incredible and utterly crazy it may seem, Hillman has acknowledged that he got the help of his daughter, a schoolgirl, to write these 'memos' whose subject was no less than the future of the world, and the waging of war in the Middle East by the one and only superpower on the planet! Perle was not – according to Hillman – apprised of these letters when they were sent to the Saudis. But he later learnt about them, and made no comment.

The day after the second memo, a lunch was organized in Marseilles, with Khashoggi, Zuhair, Perle and Hillman. Perle constituted the 'bait' – in the term used by Khashoggi to the journalist Seymour Hersh. Zuhair wanted to discuss the financial set-up designed to benefit Trireme, but above all he wanted to talk about the future of Iraq. Perle started the discussion by explaining, surprisingly enough, that he was above mere money and was 'more involved in politics'.[6]

While Perle acknowledges that he was never aware of the memos reaching Zuhair, and that he showed little interest in the solutions proposed by the latter, it is difficult to understand what was the reason for this encounter. According to Prince Bandar bin Sultan, the permanent ambassador of Saudi Arabi to the United Nations and the son of the Defence Minister Khaled bin Sultan, 'there has to be deniability, and a cover story – a possible peace initiative in Iraq – is needed. I believe the Iraqi events are irrelevant. A business meeting took place.'[7] Zuhair certainly did understand this. And the investment in question did not take place.

But then the affair assumed a completely unexpected dimension. The schoolgirl's memos were picked up by the Saudi daily *Al Ayat*, published in London, one month after the aforementioned conversation between Perle and Zuhair, in an article evocatively entitled: 'Washington Offers to Avert War in Return for an International Agreement to Exile Saddam'.[8] Further on, *Al Ayat* explained that Perle and other officials had held 'secret meetings' to avoid war.

A few days later the Lebanese paper *Al Safir* went and published a translation of the memos written by Miss Hillman and her father, attributing them directly to Richard Perle.

This whole affair clearly shows to what extent a muddling of different domains can take an unexpected and unpredictable turn when financial interests and political power get embroiled in unnatural relations with each other. Perle is a particularly outspoken critic of Saudi Arabia within the administration he supposedly serves, but he does not hesitate, through the societies of which he is a member, to approach investors from this same country for money. Of course, no law was broken. But the conflict of interests is evident. Hillman, an associate of Trireme and a member of the Defense Policy Board, is the most striking example, using his role as Pentagon adviser to attract potential investors by detailing the alleged 'conditions' that Saddam Hussein would have to fulfil in order to avoid war. Richard Perle, as an associate of Trireme, participated in the debate, but was cunning enough to keep an escape exit open, for example in the Saudi briefing of Murawiec.

The affair, which was disclosed by the journalist Seymour Hersh in March 2003, drew from Richard Perle a reaction that was as stupefying as it was revealing. In front of CNN cameras, in the presence of TV presenter Wolf Blitzer, the Pentagon adviser declared that Hersh was a 'terrorist'. When Blitzer, surprised at his guest's reaction, asked him to explain his remarks, Perle continued: 'Because he's wildly irresponsible. If you read the article, it's first of all impossible to find any consistent theme in it. But the suggestion that my views are somehow related to the potential for investments in homeland defense is complete nonsense.'[9]

Perle seems to have developed a strategy in which any investigation into his person or any supposition about the validity of his acts becomes a veritable attack on national security. Hersh's article was far from being libellous and indeed constituted a model of journalistic rigour, in which facts are assembled and corroborated with great precision. But it was less the form than the content which represented, in Perle's eyes, an unforgivable act of betrayal. He seems to have adopted for his own use the President's refrain when it comes to the war on terrorism: 'You're either for us, or against us.' The context of war seems to him a sufficient justification for silencing all criticism, even when it reveals an obvious conflict of interests.

And in the case of Richard Perle these are numerous. In February 2000 he was appointed director of Autonomy, a British hi-tech company which in particular works on intercepting computer information. Autonomy recently won, in the framework of the war of terrorism, an important contract with the US Department of Homeland Security. This company also works with the US army and US navy, as well as with the Australian Air Force. As always, Perle does not cross the boundaries of legality, insofar as the Defense Policy Board that he chaired until the beginning of 2003 (he is still a member) is a *consultative* organization of the Pentagon. By virtue of this position on the margins of the administration, Perle is not subject to the same constraints as the direct members of the Bush administration. But his influence, which extends far beyond the limits of his official appointments, has led the independent watchdog, the National Association of Pension Funds, to ask questions about the status of Richard Perle within this company. NAPF has declared that it envisaged recommending shareholders of this firm to abstain if the hawk-turned-businessman kept his position in Autonomy after the expiry of his current mandate.

A 750,000-Dollar Contract

On the other hand, Perle has obtained a 'consultancy' contract with the bankrupt American firm Global Crossing, so as to make it easier for it to be bought up by the Hong Kong company Hutchinson Whampoa. The reason is simple. Global Crossing has at its disposal a gigantic network of fibre optics, which are used by American Defense and its different agencies. Hutchinson Whampoa belongs to Li Ka-shing, the wealthiest man in the former British colony, whose links with the Communist regime in Beijing have been established for a long time. The White House has no desire to see this highly sensitive system of communication getting into the hands of a regime still considered as hostile.

Enter Richard Perle, with a contract for 750,000 dollars, 600,000 of which depend on the sale being approved by the

American authorities. In a memo dated 7 March 2003, it was emphasized that his position as chairman of the Defense Policy Board conferred on him a 'unique perspective on and intimate knowledge of' the security and defence problems that would be raised by the Foreign Investments Committee and that would be capable of blocking the sale to Hutchinson Whampoa.[10]

Perle told the *New York Times* that the document had been drawn up by lawyers and that he had not noticed that phrase. Later on he retracted his statement, declaring that the phrase could be found in a previous version, that he had crossed it out, but that someone had put it back into the final document, without him noticing it when he read it over one last time.

In fact, whatever the ultimate truth behind this notorious phrase, it is evident that his post as Pentagon adviser and his semi-official status as the ideologue of the neo-conservatives have played a determining role in the choice of Perle to conduct these negotiations. This man declared, for instance, on the subject of power and business, that he found it wrong that a man could leave an official post only to be found the very next day negotiating with the government of which he had been part. And yet Richard Perle, for his part, will not even wait to have left his job on the Defense Policy Board before sharing his 'intimate knowledge' of defence problems with his clients.

At the beginning of 1989 the *Wall Street Journal* had already revealed the existence of a company representing the Turkish government and called International Advisers Inc. (IAI), whose objective was to 'promote the objective of US–Turkish defence industrial cooperation'.[11] Turkey, let us recall, is Israel's most reliable military ally in the region.

Richard Perle has, once again, denied any such direct link, explaining that he was merely an 'adviser' to the IAI. This is true insofar as this company was registered by another current hawk: Douglas Feith. IAI brought in several hundreds of thousands of dollars for this former special adviser of Perle, as it did for his former law practice, Feith & Zell, which includes an impressive business enterprise among its clients: Northrop Grunman. This aeronautics constructor manufactures B2 bombers, F18 fighter-bombers, and pilotless drones – all used to a massive extent in Iraq.

Anyone who scrutinizes the fortunes built up by the hawks during the years preceding their appointments is struck by their closeness to the arms or military technology industries. No administration in the past ever had such close links. The key men in the Pentagon or the White House all have a past linking them to the country's industrial–military complex. Those who decided on the staggering increase in the American military budget headed or advised companies that are today its principal beneficiaries.

Northrop Grunman was not merely a client of Douglas Feith's firm. The current Air Force Secretary, James Roche, was its former vice-president. Paul Wolfowitz, no. 2 at the Pentagon, as well as Dov Zackheim, appointed Controller at the Department of Defense, were both remunerated by Northrop Grunman as 'consultants' before their appointments, without my having been able to discover what exactly they were paid for.

Karl Rove, a highly important presidential adviser, was for his part a shareholder in Boeing – and it is often forgotten that a major part of this company's activities are located in the military domain. Thus Boeing manufactures the Apache AH-64 'tank hunter' helicopters, as well as the JDAM guidance systems which transform standard shells into high-precision bombs. But Karl Rove was not the only member of the team in power to be close to Boeing.

Richard Armitage, Deputy Secretary of State, was a consultant for the firm before joining the Bush administration. He was also a consultant for Raytheon, which produces BGM-109 cruise missiles, known as Tomahawks, as well as the 'Bunker Buster' bombs GBU-28, used in Iraq to pierce the armour plating of bunkers.

The other American arms giant, Lockheed Martin, has even closer relations with the Bush administration, since the Vice-President's wife, Lynn Cheney, the real firebrand of the ultra-conservatives, was on the board of this company until February 2001.

10

Cheney and Company

Indeed, the Vice-President constitutes a flagrant example of this closeness, this intimacy even, between the political and the military–industrial powers. Unlike Richard Perle, Paul Wolfowitz, Douglas Feith or Elliott Abrams, Dick Cheney has no particular link with Israel. But his career is characterized by a marked extremism, especially as concerns American domestic politics. In 1988 he was one of the four members of Congress to vote against the ban on the most dangerous categories of weapons. Three years earlier, he had also voted against the ban on armour-piercing bullets, thereby rendering the bullet-proof jackets worn by the police completely useless against anyone with this kind of weapon. In 1984 he refused to allocate a budget of 65 million dollars (that of the Pentagon is close to 400 *billion*!) to protect battered women and reduce violence between married couples. Everyone remembers how, a few days after the horrors of 11 September, George Bush in New York put his arm round a fireman on the verge of tears, and didn't have the words to express all his admiration for their heroism and their sacrifices. Well, his Vice-President had, in the past, voted twice against granting a bonus of 50,000 dollars for the widows and orphans of firemen killed on service (as well as members of the police).

Dick Cheney's past is littered with votes and decisions that are deeply embarrassing. He refused in turn to endorse food programmes for the most deprived children in America (1986), to create a data bank on the successive statistics relating to racist crimes, and to grant food support to the elderly (1987).

In the environmental domain, Dick Cheney sings the same old song, voting against several laws for the protection of water, air, or animal species that risk extinction. But his choices, this time, have not been dictated by his rather idiosyncratic political convictions. For the Vice-President is an oil man.

The Vice-President and Iraq

After leaving the Pentagon, which he headed from March 1989 to January 1993, under the orders of the current President's father, Dick Cheney became head of that giant of the oil industry, Halliburton. This company deserves a story all to itself, given the history of its variegated, murky, and intrigue-filled activities, which link American political leaders at the highest level to the business world and foreign governments, whether in Africa, Asia, the former Soviet Union, or the Gulf.

In order to understand the career of Dick Cheney, we need to understand Halliburton. This is not just one but several companies, working in domains as diverse as pipelines, the construction of military prisons, or the logistics of American bases in Afghanistan, to mention just one country. It negotiates, via its subsidiaries, with the governments of countries that the Bush administration describes as 'terrorists', as well as with others that count among the worst dictatorships on the planet. And this was true even when Dick Cheney was running it.

Halliburton is a hydra, with not just two heads, but four, or five, or ten. Several of its numerous subsidiaries shed a harsh light on the profound disparity between official language and business realities.

Cheney was appointed to run Halliburton in 1995. This company was a major player in oil drilling and transport, so Iraq constituted a potential client, despite the embargo. When asked about this in 2000, he declared to ABC-TV, 'I had a firm policy that we would not do anything in Iraq, even arrangements that were supposedly legal.'[1]

What a pity that Saddam Hussein's Iraq was not informed about this 'firm policy': in 1998 Dick Cheney was running Halliburton, when it proceeded to buy up Dresser Industries Inc., which itself had already proceeded to the sale of oil equipment to Baghdad, via a complex set-up involving the subsidiaries of joint ventures created with another company, Ingersoll-Rand Co.

Not content with proceeding to buy up companies that had worked with Iraq in the past, in flagrant contradiction to his ideas and his speeches, Dick Cheney did not put a stop to these commercial activities that he considered so reprehensible: from the first quarter of 1997 to the start of 2000, the two subsidiaries of Halliburton, Dresser Rand and Ingersoll Dresser Pump Co., sold reprocessing pumps, spare parts for the oil industry, and pipeline equipment to Iraq, all via French subsidiaries. France, let us remind ourselves, is accused by the Americans of only defending its own interests in Iraq, as against the democratic war advocated by Dick Cheney.

As the height of cynicism, Ingersoll Dresser Pump even tried to sign a contract – which was blocked by the then American administration – aimed at repairing an oil terminal destroyed by American forces during the first Gulf War, under the command of the same Dick Cheney who was Secretary of Defense at the time.

But the fine declarations he uttered in 2000 on the intransigence that he was showing towards Iraq were merely electoral window-dressing for this man who is practically married to oil. Was it not the same Dick Cheney who, in 1996, during a conference on energy, was already showing his irritation at the sanctions imposed on certain regimes? 'We seem to be sanction-happy as a government', he said at an energy conference in April 1996. 'The problem is that the good Lord didn't see fit to always put oil and gas resources where there are democratic governments.'[2] The 'good Lord', summoned to the help of Halliburton...

After his declarations of total integrity, explaining that he refused, in any way whatsoever, to do business with Iraq, Dick Cheney was caught up with by reality. In particular, by a confidential United Nations report, published by the *Washington Post*, detailing the different companies involved in transactions with the Baghdad regime. Forced to acknowledge the reality, he explained that at the time the two subsidiaries had been bought up, he was not aware of their relations with Iraq. 'We inherited two joint ventures with Ingersoll-Rand that were selling some parts into Iraq,' said Cheney, 'but we divested ourselves of those interests.'[3]

Indeed – but not before December 1999 and January 2000, which allowed them nonetheless to sign almost 30 millions dollars' worth of contracts. Moreover, as for Cheney's ignorance about the activities of his subsidiaries, the former chairman of Ingersoll-Rand, James E. Perella, when questioned by the *Washington Post* on 23 June 2001, expressed strong reservations. 'Oh, definitively, he was aware of the business.'[4]

The hypocrisy of castigating the Iraqi regime and subjecting its population to a continued embargo which benefited the dictator speaks volumes about the sincerity of the Americans in their current campaign. Companies such as Halliburton contributed, via clever set-ups that involved a mixture of subsidiaries and intermediaries, to the riches that the GIs have recently been discovering, to their stupefaction, in the presidential palaces of Baghdad. From 4 billion dollars in 1997, Iraq's oil exports rose to 18 billion three years later. And this would never have been possible without the contribution of foreign technology, spare parts and components unavailable within the country.

Where there is Oil...

Dick Cheney may drape himself in the morality of the war he has been waging on behalf of democracy, but Halliburton has never hesitated to compromise with the foulest regimes on the planet, so as to mitigate the effects of the 'good Lord's' decision not to put oil in the right places. In 1997 those in charge of the Yadana project, a pipeline zigzagging its way through Burma, contacted the European Marine Service to carry out part of the work, especially in the offshore zones of the route.

The European Marine Service is, as in the case of Ingersoll-Rand, a joint venture with Halliburton. But this same route had been chosen to minimize the costs, despite the villages that it crossed and the ethnic minorities who lived in the zone. The SLORC (State Law and Order Restoration Council, the military junta in power in Rangoon) embarked on a veritable ethnic cleansing of the region, raping, massacring and enslaving the survivors so as to force them to work on the notorious pipeline. The entire history of the Burmese military regime is strewn with corpses, atrocities and ferocious repressions. Whether it is a question of ethnic minorities, students or activists, SLORC holds onto power only by murder and terror. Not that this stopped Halliburton from being well established there, from 1990, when it opened a bureau in Rangoon.

On this subject, Dick Cheney explained on CNN to Larry King, 'You have to operate in some very difficult places and oftentimes in countries that are governed in a manner that's not consistent with our principles here in the United States . . . But the world's not made up only of democracies.'[5]

Nor is it made of consistent politicians, either. What is Dick Cheney's philosophy when faced with a brutal and anti-democratic regime? The answer apparently depends on the circumstances: if you are Vice-President, you go to war with it. But if you're in business, then you do business with it.

For Dick Cheney apparently hates sanctions even more than he hates dictators. In addition, it is interesting to look at the countries whose cause seems to move the Vice-President, and to impose over them a map of world oil reserves. The Vice-President's generosity rarely oversteps these zones. He campaigned against Iran, for instance, via the Libya Sanctions Act, which seriously handicapped commercial exchanges between these countries and the United States. So what if today Iran is one of the 'axis of evil' countries and on the United States black-list, with the Marines on its borders? One incoherence more or less won't make much of a difference.

These countries have two things in common: real links with certain terrorist organizations (Hezbollah in the case of Iran, for instance), as well as (above all) astronomical quantities of oil. Let's forget about terrorism! Despite Qadaffi and the Iranian mullahs, Cheney thinks that sanctions can be lifted.

Cheney also militated in favour of Azerbaijan, all aid to which was suspended by a decision of Congress, which suspects this country of indulging in ethnic repression. This is a campaign devoid of any real proof, orchestrated by the Armenian lobby in the United States, according to Dick Cheney. Halliburton, in 1997, was very interested in this country that had been very well provided for by the 'good Lord' when it came to energy.

Nigeria is another example of this 'cooperation' with oil dictatorships. The regime is accused of favouring companies such as Halliburton, but also Shell and Chevron, through the arrest and assassination of those opposed to the disastrous consequences of oil exploitation on the environment.

USA Engage: Friends of Dictators and Oil

To gain a hearing, Dick Cheney is not alone. Under his leadership, Halliburton was an eminent member of USA Engage, a lobbying organization with the aim of persuading Congress and those in power of the inanity of sanctions and the imperious necessity of doing business with dictators. But let us be clear: the considerations put forward have nothing to do with, for example, the sufferings endured by the Iraqi people since the creation of the embargo that hit them so hard. The motives of USA Engage are not humanitarian but economic. By hiding behind a theory which has shown its limits in the past all too well, and which claims that commerce can change regimes from within and lead them gradually towards democracy, USA Engage militates for the lifting of sanctions against regimes that have made themselves guilty of human rights violations.

This vision, rather too naive to be entirely honest, that thinks it can transform tyrants into democrats (or at least get them to leave power) by the mere magic of commerce, benefits a small number of enterprises, whose interests are often linked to the destinies of authoritarian regimes in power throughout the Third World. USA Engage says that it brings together more than 600 members. In reality, the figure is much less than that of the official figure. For example, Tim Hussey, managing director of Hussey Seating of Maine, which supposedly belongs to the lobbying group, does not even know what USA Engage is.

In fact, a few big companies – mainly oil companies – pilot this organization. Jack Rafuse, the chief lobbyist of the UNOCAL firm, the petrol giant that was a major partner in talks with the Burmese military junta during the 1990s, and was then very active in the Afghanistan of the Taliban, heads the Committee on State and Local Sanctions within USA Engage, which includes among its 'real' members the firms Mobil and Texaco. These two other heavyweights have supported the Nigerian government in the United States, by trying to block the sanctions looming over it after the imprisonment of 7,000 people and the murder of the dissident Saro-Wiwa.

At their sides, apart from Halliburton, we also find Boeing, whose objective is somewhat different: the construction company wanted above all to wipe the slate clean after the massacre in Tiananmen Square, to normalize its relations with Beijing. Between 1992 and 1994, Boeing sold one in ten aeroplanes in the People's Republic of China. It was inconceivable that problems of democracy or human rights should interfere with such profitable markets.

This lobbying group, of which the business concern headed by Dick Cheney was an integral part, tried to have a law passed at the end of 1997, rendering the application of economic sanctions on a dictatorship an absolute nightmare. In fact, this law, introduced by Senator Richard Lugar and the Congressional Representative Lee Hamilton, means that 'sanctions are just fine if the economic interests of a company are threatened by intellectual property, theft or expropriation, but they should not be imposed if a dictatorship is killing its people or depriving workers of their rights', in the words of Mark Anderson, a union official at the Food and Allied Services Trades who keeps a close eye on the activities of USA Engage.[6] For Simon Billennes, who heads Franklin Research & Development Corp., an investment firm in Boston which has also followed the pressures USA Engage has brought to bear on Congress, 'if USA Engage had succeeded with these tactics during the apartheid years, Nelson Mandela might still be in prison'.[7] And everyone remembers that economic sanctions played a major role in the collapse of the white South African regime.

When we analyse with the benefit of hindsight Dick Cheney's membership of this organization, via Halliburton, the contradiction is only superficial. This man holds to a 'hands-off' policy towards the federal authority when it comes to government and political philosophy. These fierce opponents of a powerful and ubiquitous government in citizens' lives recruit the hard core of their supporters from the Midwest and in particular from southern and western states such as Texas. For Cheney, Washington must not have any control over the weapons bought by Americans, nor even the armour-piercing munitions they can bring in. Nor must it keep afloat the disinherited or the elderly, for fear of creating European-style 'charity', the current Vice-President's worst nightmare.

USA Engage shares the same philosophy: for Dick Cheney, the government must ensure a 'minimum maintenance' of the country, and above all not interfere with private business, whether it be that of companies or of individuals. Seen from this angle, Dick Cheney's 'schizophrenia', which consists of doing business with regimes that he would not hesitate to overthrow once he was in power, is self-explanatory. For the Vice-President, the private sector must be free of all constraint, so long as it does not impinge on state security: to put it more clearly, democracy and business are two dossiers that must remain strictly separate.

Kellog Brown & Root and the Army

But where is Dick Cheney in all this? He left Halliburton with around 45 million dollars in stock options, and the eternal gratitude of the company that he had guided to the uppermost echelons of power, in America as well as abroad (particularly in the Arab world). Where does his loyalty lie? In the business world, or the world of politics? If you look at the war, and the considerable risks – in terms of credibility – run by American leaders, you can easily suppose that his motivations were political through and through. But when you look at the postwar situation, things seem quite different.

The Vice-President's former company was picking up contracts of the highest importance for the reconstruction of the country at the very same time as the bombardments were continuing, and this happened in a quite unusual way. America is one of the most transparent countries on the planet, especially in invitations to tender. And yet, Halliburton did not have to face the least competition when it came to obtaining the first of these highly coveted

Iraqi markets. Why? Andrew Natsios, the head of the US Agency for International Development (USAID) tried to justify this manoeuvre: 'I mean, this is not unusual in terms of the way we're doing this, except that we speed up the process.'[8]

This way of going about things did not convince everybody, far from it: the Congressional Representative Henry Waxman (California) asked the Engineer Corps to explain their role in the Halliburton contract.

> I am writing to inquire why the administration entered into a contract potentially worth tens of millions of dollars or more with a subsidiary of Halliburton without any competition or even notice to Congress. The contract . . . has no set time limit and no dollar limit and is apparently structured in such a way as to encourage the contractor to increase its costs and, consequently, the costs to the taxpayer.[9]

In spite of these reservations, the position of Halliburton in Iraq has merely grown ever stronger. While George W. Bush declared that Iraqi petrol belonged to the Iraqis, it was learnt on 12 May that a contract reached with the army, again without any invitation to tender, gave to one of its subsidiaries, KBR, the *de facto* concession of a portion of Iraq's oil.

KBR, or Kellog Brown & Root, is a logistics company that benefits from almost symbiotic links with the American army that go back to the Vietnam War. It constitutes a sort of civilian Siamese twin brother to the military establishment. It has profited handsomely from Dick Cheney's connections during the years that the current Vice-President spent at the head of Halliburton. And even before he got involved in business: in 1992, when Dick Cheney was head of the Pentagon, he ordered a secret report for *3.9 million dollars* from Kellog Brown & Root. On what subject? To explain how private companies could ensure the logistics of American military operations. So KBR picked up almost 4 million dollars to write its own publicity!

It is hardly an exaggeration to say that everything which the army can delegate when it comes to maintenance and engineering falls to Kellog Brown & Root, both in the United States and abroad.

For example, the Guantanamo Bay prison that holds detainees suspected of belonging to Al Qaeda networks was built by KBR, as were huge numbers of American bases and military camps throughout the planet.

Its political donations are evidence of its natural inclinations, and partly explain the benevolence that the administration seems to feel towards it. Between 1999 and 2002, KBR spent around 709,320 dollars to support 'its' candidates in the country's various elections. Of this sum more than 673,000 dollars went to the Republicans.

In December 2001, just as the trauma of 11 September was plunging America into the Afghan conflict and the hunt for bin Laden, a contract was signed between the Pentagon and KBR, under the guise of a programme baptized LOGCAP, for Logistics Civil Augmentation Program. This contract had one peculiar feature – a significant one, too: it was to run for ten years and it set *no limit* to its overall costs. This contract was signed exactly one year after Cheney's return to power, after an absence of almost ten years.

It is tempting to wonder how such a generous decision was made by Cheney's administration, whose links with Halliburton and its subsidiary KBR are well known. In most cases, after all, there is nothing in economic terms which justifies the use of civilians on behalf of the military. As for the army, it cannot praise KBR too highly, especially via the Logistics Management Institute, which explains that the LOGCAP programme will employ 24 per cent fewer personnel, for a price that is 28 per cent lower to what military personnel would have cost themselves, if they had been assigned to the same tasks.

This is highly doubtful. A 'private' contract to provide operational support had, for instance, been presented to Congress in 1996 with a budget of 191.6 million dollars. But finally, the following year, it had exploded, eventually reaching 461.5 million dollars.

In February 2002 KBR had to pay 2 million dollars in damages after the Department of Justice had accused it of fraud against the government. One member of the firm had explained how KBR had deliberately 'inflated' its estimate for over 200 military projects. The firm had, according to the same man, presented a price list for over 30,000 products, and the total proposed was ratified by army officials. They then signed a 'working agreement' which gave not the slightest detail of the materials used. Of the 30,000 products that the military expected to see in the work done, a great number were never purchased. In fact, the army had signed an 'agreement' which, from a legal point of view, made no mention of the first list, considered as null and void even if it had served to justify the fee for the estimate.

Michael Hirst, of the Sacramento prosecutor's office, declared on this subject, 'whether you characterize it as fraud or sharp business practice, the bottom line is the same, the government was not getting what it paid for'.[10]

Thanks to this operation, KBR had succeeded in obtaining the agreement of its 'client' to carry out electrical repairs in a Californian base, at a cost of 750,000 dollars, whereas, according to T. C. McIntosh, a Pentagon investigator, it only really cost 125,000 dollars.

In 1997 the General Accounting Office (GAO), the audits office of the American Congress, declared that the absence of army monitoring of the contract agreed with KBR in former Yugoslavia had greatly increased the latter's profits. At this period, let us recall, the current Vice-President was directing the parent company, Halliburton.

The GAO report explained in particular that, at that time, KBR had been authorized by the army to import American plywood at a price of 85.98 dollars per unit, on the pretext that the company had no time to stock up in Europe, where the same material cost 14.06 dollars.

Since the start of the war on terrorism, with no ceiling being set to the costs of the aforementioned LOGCAP, business is excellent for KBR. The Pentagon has recently announced that the firm was now running food supplies, fuel and electricity at the Khanabad air base, in Uzbekistan, where in Halliburton's own terms they employ Uzbeks, paying them in accordance with local laws and customs. We knew that it was common practice, in certain countries, to pay people badly, but we learn from Halliburton that it is also a 'custom'. According to the *New York Times*, which questioned those responsible for the operation, it

would cost, for 2003, '10 per cent to 20 per cent more than if
military personnel were used'. According to Lieutenant-Colonel
Clay Cole, in charge of the contract for the army, the costs of the
work awarded to KBR could 'dramatically escalate' if they were
not kept under surveillance.[11] But, according to the same officer,
adequate control measures were put in place. Between KBR and
the army, those two long-time partners, it seems that mutual trust
is the order of the day.

But the military is right to be wary. For the subsidiary of
Halliburton, the opportunities still to come in this region may turn
out to be quite colossal. We need to remember that in the Balkans
KBR had sneaked in through the back door, only to carve out a
lion's share for itself. Its initial contract with the army in the zone
of former Yugoslavia was less than 4 million dollars. But it ended
with agreements worth several billions.

This new practice – sub-contracting a part of the army's remit to
private firms, even in a war zone, seems to be almost exclusively
reserved to KBR. And it is becoming increasingly possible to speak
of a veritable 'privatization of the army'. The report of Major
Maria Dowling, published by an Air University at Maxwell Air
Force Base (Alabama), shows how KBR employees can end up
living with soldiers, wearing the uniforms of the American army,
and bearing arms – for their own security in unstable zones.

According to another research report from the same university,
the number of these civilian/military hybrids is growing rapidly,
since, from a ratio of one to every fifty soldiers, it rose to one for
every ten during the Balkans conflict. As far as current operations
are concerned, the great number of data still classified as defence
secrets prevents me from providing a reliable estimate. But it is
reasonable to assume that the ratio of private personnel to military has further decreased.

Apart from the obvious, and quite real, risk of seeing an army
'infiltrated' by private societies, the lack of professionalism of civilian employees poses serious dangers, due to the absence of adequate training and preparation.

For example, in the desert of Saudi Arabia, the army discovered
with consternation that non-military drivers, engaged in the
country, had stopped at the side of the road and were quietly

cooking their meals with a bottle of propane, only a few metres away from their lorries that were stuffed full of explosives and munitions.

In addition, if the army does not leave its men behind it, business concerns have no compunction in doing so, even in war zones. In 1994, when KBR left Somalia at the same time as the American forces, after the extent of its operations in that country had – briefly – made it the biggest employer in the whole African continent, the local employees who had been so useful as cheap labour were purely and simply left to their own devices, with the unenviable label of 'collaborators' which must have constituted an inevitable death sentence. The future seems radiant for KBR, thanks both to the American army and to the reconstruction of Iraq.

KBR, after all, was not a subsidiary annexed to Halliburton, consigned to oblivion and mentioned from time to time in board meetings. It counted at that time for a third of the group's revenues, and this proportion is certainly increasing, insofar as Halliburton is undergoing considerable set-backs on the stock market, whereas KBR is clinching one new market after another.

A Hasty Departure?

While heading Halliburton, Dick Cheney was presiding hardly less directly over the destinies of its subsidiary. He was already considered, quite justifiably, as a priceless asset for the group, thanks to his multiple contacts in governments throughout the planet. 'He would be able to open doors around the world and to have access practically anywhere', declared Thomas Cruikshank, ex-chairman of Halliburton, who signed on Dick Cheney. The current chairman, David J. Lesar, also says, 'If I went to Egypt or Kuwait or Oman alone, I could see the Energy Minister. But when Cheney and I went to Oman, we would see the sultan. When we went to Kuwait, we would see the emir, and I mean it was not just a courtesy call. It was, "Let's go have tea and go off together".'[12]

And the more frequent were Dick Cheney's visits to Arab – and other – leaders, the more the company's profits continued to rise. In hardly more than a year, Halliburton's revenues experienced a

30 per cent increase. This is breathtaking if you consider that this company was already well established at the four corners of the globe and was already active on the world's main markets, whether we are talking about oil for Halliburton or civil engineering for KBR. In 1997 the increase in its share even exceeded that of the S&P index, even though that itself was still in a state of euphoria. And even if the current Vice-President has abstained from lobbying directly in government, there are figures that do not lie and that it is difficult to deny: between 1995 and 2000 the level of federal contracts was doubled in relation to the previous period, reaching the record figure of 2.3 billion dollars! But this was not all: during these five years Halliburton also obtained 1.5 billion dollars in government loans, guaranteed by the American taxpayer.

Dick Cheney seemed to have given a second wind to Halliburton, this old Texan company, known for its ultra-conservative sympathies, which, in the terms of Fred Mutalibov, an analyst of the oil sector, 'was a neat company that lacked an international reputation'.[13] Its new boss had given it that, and at the same time a considerably higher profile on government markets.

But this incredible fairytale was to be short-lived as far as Halliburton was concerned. In 1998 Dick Cheney decided to proceed with the acquisition of Dresser, which I mentioned a little earlier, as it was one of the American companies to have done business indirectly with Iraq. Dresser, which in 1948 had been George Bush's first employer, was working in more or less the same sectors as Halliburton. This acquisition produced a giant worth 17 billion dollars and with 103,000 employees: the biggest oil service firm on the planet.

The idea was twofold: it consisted first and foremost in getting rid of a potential rival, then in profiting from the sectors in which the capabilities of Dresser were greater than those of Halliburton. The weakest departments would for their part be purely and simply closed.

Everything was for the best in the best of all possible worlds, until the price of a barrel of crude oil unfortunately decided to plunge: Halliburton went from a profit of 772 million dollars in 1997 to a loss of 15 million the following year. Dick Cheney adopted a reassuring tone with his employees, explaining that this 'streamlining' would be minimal and that it was out of the question to apply the policy of brutal dismissal that was current in other businesses. Then he gave several thousand of them the sack in less than a year.

In tandem with this decision, characteristic of the Vice-President's natural generosity, a change in the accounts structure of Brown & Root (the old name of KBR before the arrival of Dresser's subsidiary, Kellog), was to turn Dick Cheney's future upside down. And even create the first scandal of the Bush administration in which he would be the direct target.

Until 1997, most of the contracts of Brown & Root stipulated that the client would incur all the risks if the estimate was overrun. But after this date, the firm abandoned this increasingly obsolete practice and opted for fixed contracts. This novelty implied that all overruns must be negotiated with the client, which most often led to interminable arguments and dithering. Now, Halliburton's policy consisted in not recording revenues until the disputes in question had been settled. But this cautious measure was dropped in the third quarter of 1998, when the economic situation was deteriorating. Coincidence, or a desire to camouflage the losses so as to protect the share price?

In May 2002 the *New York Times* published the confidential remarks of two Dresser officials who stated that 'two former executives of Dresser Industries, which merged with Halliburton in 1998, said that they concluded after the merger that Halliburton had instituted aggressive accounting practices to obscure its losses.'[14] These changes in bookkeeping methods – even if not illegal – allowed Halliburton to 'grant' itself an income of 89 million dollars, without even declaring this modification to the Securities and Exchange Commission, before the beginning of 2000. This same SEC opened an inquiry on the matter in 2002.

But Halliburton was literally brought to its knees by a much more unexpected problem, and one that was completely outside its control: asbestos. In 1998 Cheney knew there was a problem linked to this product in Halliburton and Dresser. What he did not know was that a company sold by Dresser in 1992 would turn against the latter to pay its own plaintiffs. And that Halliburton, Dresser's owner, would thereby be held responsible for it.

This news came at the worst possible moment: in 1997 the United States Supreme Court decided that the victims of asbestos could no longer be classed in groups since each case was unique. From that moment, the number of individual cases brought to court exploded, dragging Halliburton down into a veritable financial abyss. The number of complaints lodged against the group rose from 70,500 in 1998 to 274,000 at the end of 2001.

At the start of 2002, when Harbison Walker, Halliburton's underwriter, itself went bankrupt, Wall Street started to ask whether the oil giant would survive the crisis.

Thereafter, Dick Cheney's departure to join George Bush's presidential campaign in 2000 was surrounded in controversy. Although there has been no serious allegation of wrongdoing, the fact remains that, through luck or shrewdness, Cheney made a profit of 18.5 million dollars by selling his shares for more than 52 dollars each. Some sixty days later, Halliburton 'surprised investors with a warning that its engineering and construction business was doing much worse than expected, driving shares down 11 per cent in a day. About the same time, it announced it was under a grand jury investigation for overbilling the government.'[15]

Cheney, then, sold his shares at the very best moment, getting rich from a group whose remaining shareholders were to face heavy losses. As it happens, though, Cheney was under no obligation to sell at that precise moment. Members of a US administration are obliged to liquidate their holdings on taking office. If Cheney had held on to his shares, as he was entitled to do, until January of the following year, then he would have sustained a heavy loss. By selling some months beforehand, as he joined the presidential campaign in August 2000, he became a very wealthy man.

This fortune, extracted from a giant enterprise in decline, is not even justified by the business talents of the current Vice-President. His almost limitless contacts, across the entire planet, had made him a major intermediary – a middleman capable of establishing links between governments and big multinational companies, as

well as being someone who was able to help get difficult contracts
signed thanks to his immense experience of negotiation.

But as a manager, he did not shine. At least not enough to earn
himself 30 million dollars. According to James Wicklun, an analyst
at the Bank of America Securities, 'He came in at a time when
any okay manager could ride the cyclical wave.'[16]

Halliburton and the Russians

Dick Cheney surfed on waters that turned out to be, on certain
occasions, distinctly murky. As when Halliburton obtained, at the
beginning of 2000, a public loan of 489 million dollars, guaranteed by the taxpayer, to a Russian company with a more than
dubious reputation.

Halliburton launched a lobbying campaign vis-à-vis the
Export–Import bank, the American organization that issues this
kind of loan, despite the protests of the State Department, which
considered that such an agreement was going 'against the national
interest' of the United States.[17] The Russian firm at the heart of
the debate, Tyumen Oil, was lumbered with a dodgy past, though
this did not discourage Dick Cheney and the other bosses at
Halliburton. The firm BP Amoco, the biggest gas and oil producer
in the United States, claimed that following a series of frauds and
more than dubious practices, Tyumen had quite simply stolen one
operation in which the Anglo-American giant possessed an important stake. According to the Centre for Public Integrity (CPI),
which publishes inquiries into dysfunctions in American public
life, and which took an interest in Tyumen during 2000, Tyumen's
roots 'go deep into a network of corruption linked to the KGB
and the [former] Communist Party, but also to drug trafficking
and money from organized crime'. For Tyumen's representative in
the United States, the famous firm of lawyers Akin & Gump, such
remarks are 'off the mark'.[18] The fact remains that the parent
company to which Tyumen belongs, Alfra Group, is often
described as having close links with organized crime. Nonetheless,
as is often the case in Russia, nothing can be proved.

But Dick Cheney's support for this company was rewarded,
even if the aspiring president George W. Bush was promising on

his web site, a few months later, to redirect aid, loans and investments to the Russian people, and not to the bank accounts of corrupt officials. Indeed, James C. Langdon Jr, one of the directors of Akin & Gump, was one of Bush's 'Pioneers'.[19] This is the term used, among Republicans, to refer to the elite of donors who give over 100,000 dollars to support the future president's campaign.

But such sums are rarely handed out just because the donors like the candidate. The 'Pioneers' gain an almost direct access to the White House, and considerable lobbying power. This is a strong point when it comes to defending a disgraced Russian business concern, which is hoping to notch up a few more points for respectability in the United States.

The True Face of 'Iraqi Freedom'

So Dick Cheney is an oil man. He goes wherever the black gold can be found, despite the mistakes made by the good Lord who did not always put it where he should have. Democracy, or indeed the environment (his 'plan' for energy and oil exploration had been a real ecological scandal, which embarrassed the administration until 11 September overshadowed it) are not so much problems forced to take a back seat: they are completely absent from his system of ideas when oil interests are mentioned. When he occupies a government post, things are hardly different. Remember the contempt with which he treated the Kyoto agreement on the reduction of gases leading to the greenhouse effect (decisions on energy have always fallen within Cheney's remit in this administration). Remember too that, as a Congressional Representative, before entering the first Bush administration, Cheney voted against pretty much every law on environmental protection – not out of sadism, but merely because these same laws were in flagrant contradiction with the interests of the big oil groups that he has always mixed with.

And democracy? In the different posts he has occupied, Cheney has carved out some solid personal friendships throughout the entire Gulf region, especially in the small emirates so dear to him, and where he is so cordially received. Now, Saudi Arabia, Oman, Kuwait, Abu Dhabi and Qatar are far from being democracies: the king, or the sultan or the emir concentrates all power on himself in these countries without the least opposition, women don't have the vote, and dissidence is totally absent. Even if 11 September turned the existing order upside down, Cheney was these regimes' man in the White House.

'The most incredible thing about it', a highly placed official in the State Department told me,

> is that the collusion between state business and private business is completely obvious. When you see an Iraqi worker explaining how Kellog Brown & Root has come to get a pumping station going again at Um Qasr, when this company was still run by Cheney less than three years ago, you think you must be dreaming! This war of liberation is taking fewer and fewer precautions with its image, it seems to me. First they talked about weapons of mass destruction, links with terrorism, then, finally, they content themselves with occupying the country and getting it to pump up oil. There's no doubt about it, the everlasting paranoia of Europeans about US imperialism now has a basis in fact.

The lack of clear political direction is real enough, and the conflict that has just come to an end can be explained in terms of two radically different philosophies. In fact, Baghdad was attacked for any number of reasons, except perhaps for the reasons that are actually given.

In the clan of the pro-Israeli hawks, 11 September and the war on terror represented a real 'opportunity' to put into practice, without the least modification, the policies they had long advocated. And as explanation they brandished, in no particular order, bin Laden, weapons of mass destruction, and Al Qaeda's links with Saddam Hussein. In reality, the war in Iraq represents the first step in the policy of the neo-conservatives in the Middle East, as their reports explained throughout the 1990s. It is also explicable by their fierce determination to contribute to Israel's regional security, via the gradual weakening of its enemies, such as Iraq and Syria, to the profit of allies such as Jordan.

Even if these objectives are radically different, Dick Cheney fully subscribes to the reshaping of the Middle East which is taking place today, on the self-interested advice of the hawks. Israel is not a major preoccupation of the Vice-President – at least not in the passionate way it preoccupies Perle, Wolfowitz, Feith or Abrams. On the other hand, the lasting and exclusive establishing of American oil companies in a country which could potentially become the second producer in the region is more than enough to allure him.

Neither of the two groups is being honest. Those who now claim to be avenging the victims of 11 September and hunting down the terrorist networks have embarked on a war which serves their respective interests and strategies, utilizing this drama as a pretext, knowing that it cannot be questioned. The hawks represent the interests of those who think that Israel will triumph only by force. Cheney represents the oil giants and, together with his wife, the American extreme right (he is, for instance, one of fiercest opponents of abortion, even in the case of incest or rape), engaged in an unnatural alliance with the hardliners in Jerusalem. The most striking aspect of all this, at the present time which marks a turning point of the first importance in the history of our world, is this collusion between two schools of thought that were originally poles apart, and that are finally finding themselves united on an improbable battlefield: Iraq.

Dick Cheney's wheeling and dealing, his closeness to Halliburton and American oil groups, is probably not behind the overthrow of Saddam Hussein. This was clearly the doing of the hawks, who demonstrated to the American President that the time had come to restore the greatness of America, to change its environment and, in particular, that of the Gulf. This was something the hawks had been dreaming of for years, and this new-style Republican administration, naturally inclined to unilateral decisions, was entirely happy to listen to them.

But if Dick Cheney was not behind this war, he was probably partly behind the way events have recently turned out. What had been presented as an attempt to democratize Iraq is starting to look in part like a tragic farce: order is not established in the towns, but they are already busy repairing the oil pumps. Hospitals don't work, but KBR has already extinguished the fires in the oil wells. The whole reality of the conflict is starting to become clear: a neutralized Iraq, placed under the supervision of (exclusively American) oil companies that are already in the process of getting themselves firmly established.

A discrepancy between official language and reality? What is so surprising about the discovery that Dick Cheney was the head of a group that was doing business with Iraq, Iran and Libya? A group paid by Baghdad before its managing director became Vice-President and decided to topple that very same regime. As far as the members of the Bush administration are concerned, one more contradiction will make little difference, given how tightly interwoven money and politics are, at every level of power.

11

A Corrupt Administration?

In this respect, another member of the present administration is a textbook case, so emblematic is he of the wheeling and dealing that prevails with impunity in Washington today. 'The honourable Mr White', as the web site of the White House describes him, was appointed by George Bush as Deputy Secretary of the Army. We can learn two things from this army man. First and foremost, the past is of no importance when you have a sufficiently powerful protector in the administration. In addition, the ethical code inherent in official functions can be seriously transgressed, even if the affair becomes public, without bringing down grave sanctions.

Thomas White's past does indeed overstep the boundaries of controversy. In 1990, when Brigadier General, he left the army – where he had served with distinction in combat during the Vietnam War – to join the ranks of the firm Enron which later became notorious as the origin of one of the biggest financial scandals on the planet.

This man, who promised to establish 'sound business practices' in the Pentagon's commercial negotiations,[1] is probably the least well placed to make such declarations. Within Enron, Thomas White was in charge of a division called Enron Energy Services (EES), looking after big maintenance and energy supply contracts. In fact, the structure of this company and the way it rewarded its officials were totally deceitful. A contract for electricity supply signed for fifteen years, for example, in no case allowed the total profits of this period to be estimated in advance. You would have had to be able to anticipate a whole jumble of factors: the price of oil, government expenditure, the degree and rapidity of the liberalization of energy markets, not only in one but several states.

In fact, it was a matter of guesswork pure and simple, which could be based on no rational foundation.

Nonetheless, officials were paid on the basis of altogether imaginary extrapolations into the future. The contracts, even if only a tiny proportion of the overall sum had been paid in, were considered profitable during the first ten or fifteen years, and the managers were paid immediately, in respect of these totally illusory gains.

As in all 'pyramids', the system worked so long as new contracts kept coming in, with each one paying the commission of the previous one. Eventually, it was the whole edifice which collapsed. 'It became obvious that EES had been doing deals for two years and was losing money on almost all the deals they had booked,' declared one of its employees, Margaret Ceconi, in an e-mail to Enron bosses warning them of the situation, explaining that losses of more than 500 million dollars had in this way been concealed within the EES.[2]

The group's bankruptcy, which came about shortly afterwards, enabled the energy giant to protect itself from the incredible sum of debts built up by the man whom the White House put in charge of a budget of several tens of billions of dollars. White maintains that 'EES was a great business . . . there were no accounting irregularities that I was aware of'.[3] Either he was aware of the manipulations taking place, and he is guilty of fraud, or these operations really did go over his head and his incompetence will be a real handicap for the land army of which he is now in charge. In either case, the situation is more than worrying.

But beyond this gigantic manipulation, Thomas White also used his connections in the army to favour Enron in the negotiation of military contracts.

In 1999 a contract worth 25 million dollars was obtained by the firm to ensure the energy supply (gas and electricity) of Fort Hamilton, near Brooklyn. The conditions in which the invitation to tender was made recall the award of the first Iraqi markets to Halliburton.

Fort Hamilton is a base of the land army, the body in which White passed his entire military career, and where his contacts are best-established.

Enron obtained an exemption from the rules on security and environmental protection required by the state of New York, delivered by the NY State Public Service Commission, with the support of the army. Curiously, this exemption was granted to this firm alone: its main rival in negotiations, Con Edison, had to fulfil these extremely constraining, and above all extremely onerous, supplementary measures – which meant they lost the deal.

When you realize that Thomas White led the Fort Hamilton negotiations for Enron from beginning to end, you may well start to wonder about this strange exemption.

'Fort Hamilton was supposed to be the very first example of how privatization could work,' declares Timothy Mills, a Washington lawyer involved in lobbying for energy companies vis-à-vis the army. 'In the end, it had become an example of how everything could go wrong.'[4]

It sometimes seems as if the whole business was set up purely and simply to discourage invitations to tender to Enron's competitors. So, in its conditions the army stipulated that the base's generators would have to be acquired by the firm that won the contract. This was a sticking point, as it entailed considerable fiscal burdens, making the deal less attractive and raising the estimate. And while negotiating the final clauses of the contract with Enron, the army went back on its decision and accepted a leasing formula which exempted the company from a whole variety of different expenses.

The Pentagon is a notoriously opaque organization when it comes to invitations to tender and the acquisition of different equipment; overcharging is common practice, and the controls particularly lax. Sharp practice on estimates, prices and services is not exactly new, but it would be especially serious if Thomas White, who is responsible for bigger and bigger military budgets, were to be involved.

Despite a history that could not be more disastrous, despite the fact that he presided over the destinies of a body which built up losses of nearly 500 million dollars, White was not reprimanded. In fact, he left Enron with a real fortune: on entering the Bush administration, he declared stocks and stock options of a value between 56 and 130 million dollars. Following the collapse of

Enron's prices, he publicly complained that he had endured substantial financial losses, since he managed to get 'only' 12 million
dollars out of it. But the different systems of compensation, salary
and 'bonus' enabled him to pick up a total of almost 31 million
dollars. For a former brigadier general-turned-businessman who
has only one failure after another to his credit, this can all the
same be considered a good rate of pay.

Like all the Enron bosses who were the only ones to grow fat
on the beast's carcass, White's earnings are already rather disturbing. One may well ask what was George Bush's aim in
appointing a man with such a dubious financial past. But the
White 'affair' is far from ending there.

In January 2002, several months after the Deputy Secretary had
revealed the staggering degree of his fortune, the Senate Committee on Armies learnt that White had accepted a private income
coming partly from Enron, violating the procedures that obliged
the Secretary to free himself from any financial dependence.
Senators Carl Levin and John Warner declared, 'We do not believe
that your actions satisfied the requirements of this committee.'[5]
This is a euphemism, if you remember that one month later, these
same investigators discovered 50,000 shares deposited, to the
value of 1 million dollars, in a investment fund in 1996, concealed
by White at the time he took up office. Yet the Secretary had
signed a document obliging him to free himself from any ties that
might constitute a conflict of interests between his new position
and his old one.

But, in a manoeuvre that was really quite paradoxical if he
wanted to avoid such conflicts, White kept regular and close contacts with the men in charge of Enron.

Public Citizen, an independent watchdog that keeps a check on
morality in public life, has asked for explanations on the subject
of twenty-nine discussions and conversations with Enron bosses,
at a time when the Deputy Secretary was already in post in the
Bush administration (and was earning from this company both a
stake, via his 50,000 shares, and a paid income).

'That's how Washington works. You keep passing the buck from
private to public, and you yourself move from one to the other in

the course of your career', I was told by a high-ranking official in the State Department. 'But, and this is the problem with this administration in many areas, things are so flagrant that they even shock the old stagers [in politics] in the federal capital.' For White was not punished, or stripped of his functions. This remarkable indulgence, as we shall be seeing later, constitutes a quite unprecedented feature of American politics, but it has not calmed his feverish desires – far from it. When he was already in post, White purely and simply asked for an army plane to travel to Colorado with his wife, so as to sign the purchase of a mountain chalet belonging to the couple, for the modest sum of 6.5 million dollars! According to the State Department official I quoted earlier, 'you're used to this kind of thing with African or South American leaders. But at the same time as America is posing as a defender of democracy, our leaders are lowering themselves to practices that you only find in the corrupt dictatorships of the Third World.' White, it should be recalled, has violated two rules that were perfectly well known and clearly stated in a 1997 Defense Department directive, which notes that 'the Army Secretary is required to use military aircraft for travel on official business but specifies that authorizing officials shall ensure that an official, rather than personal, purpose is served by the travel. As a general rule, a family member is actually required to participate in an official capacity.'[6]

White, visibly feeling cornered by his own dishonesty and the strong reactions of the American public, has even declared that he was ready to leave his post if he was asked to. Unfortunately, everyone *is* asking him to, except the President. And this is probably where we find the strangest aspect of White and the various affairs he has been embroiled in, and which succeed each other without any apparent reaction from the head of the American executive.

Bush, or the Administration of Impunity

Whatever you may think of the American system, political leaders in that country are subject to a pressure that exists nowhere else and which involves the most total transparency, in private affairs, of those at the top of the political ladder. The slightest detail in their lives, their past and affairs of any kind that they may have been mixed up in, are dissected by the press and the watchdogs that keep a close eye on the morality of national public life.

Not to mention events such as Watergate, which constitute real offences that fall within the criminal domain and entail prison spells as well as fines, the watchdogs have a much wider field of investigation. If you've taken drugs at university, or slept with your secretary – all this is considered an affront to public trust, and keeps the country's leaders perched on a sort of permanent ejector seat. The most perfect and irreproachable career can sink without trace if a chink, however tiny, is discovered in the armour of the public figure. And the career of Thomas White is far, very far, from being perfect. But unlike the previous administrations, whether Republican or Democratic, this one is staying completely passive.

Harold Talbott, Air Force Secretary during the Presidency of Eisenhower in 1955, had been holding business discussions on an air force base (he at least didn't borrow a plane). The President dismissed him straight away, even though, unlike White, he had violated no law, nor any internal army directive. During Bill Clinton's Presidency, David Watkins had borrowed a helicopter to get to a golf course. He resigned the day after the scandal was made public.

Examples are legion, throughout the country's contemporary history. Even during the administration of George Bush Sr, the presidential adviser John Sununu was forced to resign after borrowing a government vehicle to get to a convention of philatelists.

But George W. Bush's administration marks a total break with the commonly accepted standards of governance and ethics. And yet there is no lack of examples. Karl Rove, the all-powerful presidential adviser who is rumoured to rival Dick Cheney in importance, has received leading figures from the Intel firm at the White House, even though he was a shareholder of this same firm. While during the two first years of Bill Clinton's Presidency, ten politicians had already resigned, the new team has lost only one member in eighteen months. Michael Parker, a second-ranking figure, was not even the victim of a watchdog or a press revelation: he was merely accused of 'disloyalty' towards the administration, the only failing which, apparently, deserves to be punished.

Undeniably, something has changed. No other administration would have kept a man like White in its ranks. According to the journalist Joshua Green, the author of a highly detailed inquiry into the Deputy Secretary that was published in the *Washington Monthly* of August 2002, the latter is more surprised than anyone to have remained in post and to have weathered the current storm.

The Bush administration has changed many things, abroad, but also in Washington, in the way it conducts the country's political affairs. The impunity that seems to be the rule today in fact conceals a deep change, where loyalty to a leader takes on greater importance, and ethics and morality are relegated to the background. Bush is at war, and war is rarely clean. What matters most on the battlefield has nothing to do with good manners, or courtesy, or principles. What matters most in combat is the loyalty of those serving you.

Bush wants loyal collaborators. He is not so bothered about the rest. In other circumstances, the watchdogs and the press would have brought him to heel. The 11 September attacks and the war on terrorism confer gigantic power on him. Today, to show doubts about the President's men is to show doubts about the President himself, as well as the entire war on terror. And the much-feared label of 'unpatriotic' hangs over anyone who pushes criticisms further.

The President and his men are at war. But they have a past, they have friends, and in many cases they have a fierce desire to get rich. Though participating in this 'war on evil', they are still old businessmen, ready to grasp the opportunities that crop up, while hiding behind their official functions. Dick Cheney, Richard Perle, Thomas White: for them, the war is a duty, but also a refuge. Perle describes over-critical journalists as 'terrorists', Dick Cheney is too powerful to have many worries about his past in Halliburton, and Thomas White hides in a tightly woven network of alliances and protections which partly explain his longevity.

His mentor is Colin Powell, the Secretary of State. Even if his star is declining, this former general remains a heavyweight on the presidential team, and in any case his son occupies an important post in the federal administration. To lift a finger against White means attacking Powell. Calvin Mackenzie, Professor of Government at Colby College, says, 'if you have a rabbi watching over you [i.e. a sponsor and protector], if you're somebody's guy, then you're much better fortified against an attack. If people start rattling your cage and your rabbi can protect you, you stick around longer.'[7]

These 'protections' and these networks are more effective in this administration than in any other.

Honesty and integrity are these days virtues that have been relegated to the background. The most important thing of all is loyalty. Colin Powell, after having tried to convince the White House to adopt a more multilateralist attitude, more open to the international community, fell in behind his boss the minute conditions demanded it. He is fulfilling his role, and Bush asks for nothing more. Since to punish White would mean indirectly attacking Powell, no senator on the Armed Forces Commission dares pursue his investigations and his sanctions any further.

A Closed and Untouchable Universe

Almost the entire current team seems to be living in a closed and untouchable universe. One that is not really opaque insofar as scandals, affairs, and conflicts of interests are revealed just as they were in previous administrations. The *New York Times* asked for the immediate resignation of Thomas White in editorials of such outspokenness that they would have produced a devastating effect under any president other than George W. Bush.

In an America that has a President who has never been inclined to subtlety, the war has created an even deeper manicheism. Whether or not the criticisms are well grounded, whether they affect individuals as such or the entire administration, makes no difference. 'For or against.' No middle ground shades of opinion. This is the way that the politics being practised today favours all the free-floating wheeling and dealing that we can see. This impunity is particularly damaging insofar as it is not content merely to absolve the wrongdoers: it encourages others to behave likewise.

Freed from many of these legal and above all moral constraints, the President thought he had his hands free to conduct the war on terrorism and to strike at America's enemies. In fact, he risks favouring the emergence of a government discredited by various blunders and by the flagrant demonstrations of its sharp business practice.

Several media channels agree that this is the case – as do (under cover of anonymity, of course) several members of the administration. But paradoxically, George Bush seems galvanized by adversity and reinforced by the idea that these many and various criticisms must not gain a hearing if his government wishes to remain strong enough to lead the combat that is its main job. 'He is a warlord more than a president', declared an officer of the DIA.[8]

Politicians such as White, nicknamed by the press the 'serial scandalizer', Cheney, or Perle (who considers Saudi Arabia as an adversary but does not hesitate to call on that country when it comes to financing his own business deals) risk endangering the objectives being pursued.

The team of hawks, which wants to reshape the Middle East through democracy, seems more and more to be relapsing into the simplistic and exaggerated behaviour imagined by of certain of its opponents.

Bush is not strengthening his team by keeping it far away from criticism and disciplinary action. He is weakening and discrediting it in the eyes of the international community. American public opinion, the only one which the President bothers about, traditionally takes little interest in foreign problems, and is not well informed about events beyond its borders. It was repeatedly drummed into the public's mind, on most TV channels, that Al Qaeda was in Iraq, that there were links between Saddam Hussein and Osama bin Laden, and that the one man's weapons would soon be being launched from the other man's country. The vast majority of Americans believed this, and they think that the world will be a safer place now that Saddam Hussein has gone.

Iraq has lost nothing by the departure of its dictator. But America has gained nothing either, except a military victory that marks the start of a long and complex future, which the world's premier nation, suffering from a commercial deficit as it is, will probably not have the means to ensure in the long term.

But Americans believe it will, and support their President, since they are at war. And yet, on 2 May 2003, George Bush stepped out of a fighter plane onto an American aircraft carrier, to declare that most military operations in Iraq were over. And this relaxes the muzzle on critics and normalizes the situation. Once the public starts paying more attention to those who make up the presidential team, and the way they have been overstepping the mark, the White House may find it increasingly difficult to hide behind current, or future, conflicts.

A Tightly Knit Administration

Whatever the clans and the rivalries within the administration, each of its members avoids pushing the others into the spotlight, in case they end up being next on the list. Many leading figures now have a past that is controversial enough to arouse fears of a chain reaction which, after the first scandal and the first sacking, would lead them to a real descent into hell. This law of silence constitutes one of the most striking aspects of the present period. And it explains why a man like Thomas White stays put. If he were to fall, the taboo would be broken, since nobody has been dismissed for two years on ethical grounds.

This group solidarity, despite the often sharp divergences of views and interests between the different figures in power, is easy to understand when you realize that this administration is almost entirely composed of old acquaintances, if not old friends.

Perle, Feith, Wolfowitz and Abrams have known each other for over thirty years. Cheney has worked for Rumsfeld. Rumsfeld was on the board of the firm ABB when it sold nuclear power plants to North Korea, which has since become a member of the axis of evil. ABB is also a member of USA Engage, one of the emblematic figures of which was Halliburton, at the time run by Dick

Cheney, along with Boeing, for which Karl Rove was even a consultant.

The links between them are a mixture of politics and private business. These links are solid and strong. When George Bush was elected, the team was ready. There was no wavering, and the cohesion of its members simply grew stronger, which was not the case in previous administrations. Joshua Green, in an article quoted above, mentions a politician who had worked with Bill Clinton, and who had this to say: 'The early Clinton years were the original amateur hour. There was no understanding of how you protect your own people, so they simply got jettisoned.'[9]

Nothing of the kind happened to the new team, which knew how to stick together and protect itself from its adversaries, and which knew better than anyone the machinery of Washington and the pitfalls to avoid. Dick Cheney and Donald Rumsfeld had been present on the national stage for decades and had built up a masterful grasp of the ambushes that lie in wait along the corridors of the White House, the Pentagon or Congress.

But their political 'trade' and the fear they feel at seeing the scandals of other people staining their own reputations do not completely explain the impunity that now reigns: the suppression in 1999 of the post of independent prosecutor leaves the current team with a freedom to manoeuvre far greater than in the past. This prosecutor, first appointed under Jimmy Carter to investigate accusations of drug taking laid against the White House Chief of Staff, Hamilton Jordan, had over the previous two decades ensured an avalanche of resignations.

The odds are that such a council would have started investigations into the various different problems that have beset the current administration. But Congress did not renew it in 1992, and reactivated it on only two occasions, in 1994 and 1999, for affairs concerning Bill Clinton's administration.

The legislative branch itself seems to be losing the aggression which, in the past, had enabled it to shed light on numerous frauds and abuses in the political class. The House of Representatives is controlled by the Republicans, whose leader Tom DeLay is a fundamentalist Christian totally in thrall to the ideas of the hawks and other supporters of the war within the administration. A man who declares, among other things, that he wants:

> to bring us back to the Constitution and Absolute Truth that has been manipulated and destroyed by a liberal worldview . . . When faced with the truth, the truth hurts. Will this country accept the worldviews of humanism, materialism, sexism, naturalism, postmodernism or any of the other -isms? Or will we march forward with a biblical worldview, a worldview that says God is our creator, that man is a sinner, and that we will save this country by changing the hearts and minds of Americans?[10]

Sharing a vision of the world and international problems that is as cut-and-dried as that of the President, he is absolutely not prepared to endorse inquiries and lawsuits that would impinge on the credibility of an administration that is entirely to his liking. As for the Senate, it is conspicuous by its absence.

So everything has combined to confer on the current leaders the impunity they seem to enjoy. Their credibility is dangerously eroded if you observe the responsibilities that America has itself decided to take on in the Middle East. It had long been claimed, in milieux that were at the time described as anti-American, that oil and business were at the heart of the Iraqi conflict. The White House explained, with some credibility, that this was not the case.

Today oil companies are digging into the country even before NGOs can become established there. In this administration, in which hawks fiercely attached to the security of Israel rub shoulders with unscrupulous and somewhat narrow businessmen such as Dick Cheney, or figures who have become quite simply unacceptable such as Thomas White, you start to wonder who can indeed still speak for Iraq's interests.

The well-known writer Norman Mailer, in his speech 'Only in America', produced a lucid and disabused account of this evolution of American power.

> In the 1930s, you could be respected if you earned a living. In the '90s, you had to demonstrate that you were a promising figure in the ranks of greed. It may be that empire depends on an obscenely

wealthy upper-upper class who, given the in-built, never-ending threat to their wealth, are bound to feel no great allegiance in the pit of their heart for democracy. If this insight is true, then it can also be said that the disproportionate wealth which collected through the '90s may have created an all-but-irresistible pressure at the top to move from democracy to empire. That would safe-guard those great and quickly-acquired gains.[11]

And what if America finished by alienating the rest of the world? This was the question that preoccupied Eric Alterman in *The Nation*. 'At some point, we may be the only ones left', Bush confided to one of his advisers. 'That's OK with me. We are America.'[12]

Notes

Chapter 1   Towards Apocalypse

1   Tony Carnes, *Christianity Today*, 2 October 2000.
2   Bush Inaugural Address to Congress on Saturday, 20 January 2001. George W. Bush took the oath of office as the forty-third President of the United States of America. His speech included the note from the Virginia statesman John Page to Thomas Jefferson, after the Declaration of Independence.
3   Agence France Presse (AFP), 3 February 2001.
4   National Prayer Breakfast at the Washington Hilton Hotel, 1 February 2001.
5   Dana Milbank and Ellen Nakashima, 'Bush team has "right" credentials', *Washington Post*, 25 March 2001.
6   'Keeping the US First: Pentagon would preclude a rival superpower', *Washington Post*, 11 March 1992.
7   Bob Woodward, *Bush at War* (Simon and Schuster, 2002).
8   Conversation with author.
9   Howard Fineman, 'Bush and God', *Newsweek*, 10 March 2003.
10   National Prayer Breakfast at the Washington Hilton Hotel, 1 February 2001.
11   Rob Boston, AFP, 3 February 2001.
12   Fineman, 'Bush and God'.
13   Matthew Engel, 'Meet the new Zionists', *The Guardian*, 28 October 2002.
14   Fineman, 'Bush and God'.
15   'Bush's Messiah Complex', *The Progressive*, February 2003.
16   Molly Ivins and Lou Dubose, *Shrub: The Short but Epic Political Life of George W. Bush* (Vintage Books, 2000).
17   Fineman, 'Bush and God'.
18   Ibid.
19   David Frum, *The Right Man* (Random House, 2003).

20 Norman Mailer, 'Only in America', speech to the Commonwealth Club of California, 20 February 2003. Full text on: *www.commonwealthclub.org/archives/03/03-02mailer-speech.html*.

21 Frum, *The Right Man*.

22 Ibid.

23 State of the Union address, at the US Capitol, 28 January.

24 Paul S. Boyer, 'When U.S. foreign policy meets biblical prophecy', *Alternet*, 20 February 2003.

25 Frum, *The Right Man*.

26 'Bush's Messiah complex', *The Progressive*, February 2003.

Chapter 2   The 'Heritage' Connection

1   Lewis F. Powell, Jr, confidential memorandum, 'Attack on American free enterprise system', *Washington Report*, 23 August 1971, *www.mediatransparency.org*.

2   Norman Mailer, 'Only in America', speech to Commonwealth Club of California, 20 February 2003.

3   Major National Conference of Conservative Foundations, at the Pierre Hotel, New York, July 2002; Robert Kuttner, 'Philanthropy and movements', *American Prospect*, 15 July 2002.

4   Will Hutton, 'Death is now the only certainty', *The Observer*, 6 May 2001.

5   Karne Rothmyer, 'Citizen Scaife', *Columbia Journalism Review*, July/August 1981.

6   'People & Events: Frederick T. Gates, 1853–1929', in 'The Rockefellers', *American Experience*, *www.pbs.org/wgbh/amex/rockefellers/index.html*.

7   Brooks Jackson, 'Who is Richard Mellon Scaife?', CNN, 27 April 1998.

8   Robert G. Kaiser and Ira Chinoy, 'Scaife: funding father of the Right', *Washington Post*, 2 May 1999.

9   People for the American Way, 'Buying a movement: national think tanks and advocacy groups', *www.pfaw.org*; 'Spinning dispensationalism', *Dubia Report*, 8 April 2002.

10 James Ridgway, 'Heritage on the Hill', *The Nation*, 22 December 1997, *www.thirdworldtraveler.com*.

11 Ibid.

12 People for the American Way, William Coors' speech to the Denver Minority Business Association, February 1984: see Adolph Coors Foundation, 'Buying a movement', *www.pfaw.org*.

13 Texas Freedom Network, *www.tfn.org.*
14 *The Philanthropy*, interview with William E. Simon, *www.philanthropyroundtable.org.*
15 People for the American Way, 'Buying a movement', *www.pfaw.org.*
16 Political Research Associates, 'The think tank Presidency', *The Public Eye, www.publiceye.org.*
17 Ibid.
18 'The charge of the think-tanks', *The Economist*, 15 February, 2003.

Chapter 3   The War of Ideas

1   Dana Milbank and Ellen Nakashima, 'Bush team has "right" credentials', *Washington Post*, 25 March 2001.
2   Noam Chomsky, interviewed by Peter Clarke on the Australian Broadcasting Corporation programme, 'Late Night Live', 16 October 2001.
3   Scott Sherman, 'David Horowitz's long march', *The Nation*, 15 June 2000.
4   Ibid.
5   Ibid.
6   David Horowitz, 'A radical's disenchantment', *The Nation*, 8 December 1979.
7   University of California, Berkeley, 1986.
8   *FrontPageMag.com.*, David Horowitz's web site.
9   Sherman, 'Long March'.
10 Ibid.
11 Ibid.
12 David Brock, *American Spectator*, March 1992.
13 David Brock, *Blinded by the Right: The Conscience of an Ex-conservative* (Three Rivers Press, 2003); excerpt in *www.randomhouse.com.*
14 Interview with Richard Mellon Scaife by John F. Kennedy Jr, *George Magazine*, January 1999.
15 Robert G. Kaiser and Ira Chinoy, 'Scaife: funding father of the Right', *Washington Post*, 2 May 1999.
16 US Supreme Court, Pentagon Event Investigation (11 September 2001).
17 Kaiser and Chinoy, 'Scaife'.
18 Ibid.
19 Mike Kress, 'Vast right wing collusion', *American Politics Journal*, 16 March 1999, *www.americanpolitics.com.*

20 Eric Alterman, 'The right books and big ideas', *The Nation*, 22 November 1999.
21 Ibid.
22 Ibid.
23 Conversation with the author.
24 People for the American Way, 'Buying a movement', *www.pfaw.org*.
25 *New York Times Magazine*, 9 October 1994.
26 Michael Powell, *Washington Post*, 17 January 1999.
27 Ibid.
28 Ben Wattenberg, *New York Times Magazine*, 23 November 1997.
29 Jon Wiener, 'Hard to muzzle', *The Nation*, 2 October 2000.
30 Lynn Cheney, *Telling the Truth* (1995).
31 Dinesh D'Souza, *The End of Racism* (Touchstone Books, 1996). See also D'Souza, 'Separation of race and state', *Wall Street Journal*, 12 September 1995 – *www.dinesh-dsouza.com*.

Chapter 4   Enter the Moonies

1 Wayne Madsen, 'Moon Shadow. The Rev, Bush and North Korea', *Counter Punch*, 14 January 2003.
2 Press statement, 15 November 1979.
3 *Washington Times*, 17 May 1992.
4 Robert Parry, 'Rev. Moon, North Korea and the Bushes', *Consortium News*, 11 October 2000.
5 Ibid.
6 Banquet to launch Moon's new publication *Tiempos del mundo* in Buenos Aires, 24 November 1996.
7 Parry, 'Rev. Moon, North Korea and the Bushes'.
8 *Unification News*, June 1997.
9 Peter McGill et al., 'Ed Schreyer and the Moonies', *Maclean's*, 23 October 1995; Andrew Pollack, 'Bush host in Japan tied to Rev. Moon', *New York Times*, 4 September 1995.
10 John Judis, *US News and World Report*, 27 March 1989.
11 Parry, 'Rev. Moon, North Korea and the Bushes'.
12 *Unification News*, June 1997.
13 'Moon's Message', Moon's web site.
14 John Judis, *US News and World Report*, 27 March 1989.
15 *www.thelionofjudah.org*.
16 Moon's 'Christian Ecumenism in the Americas', conference in Montevideo, Uruguay, 15 November 1995.

17 *www.thelionofjudah.org.*
18 Michael I. Niman, 'Bad religion', *ArtVoice*, 28 March 2002.
19 Ibid.
20 Fineman, 'Bush and God', *Newsweek*, 10 March 2003.
21 William Cook, *Counter Punch*, 22 February 2002.
22 Joe Conason and Gene Lyons, *The Hunting of the President* (St Martin's Press, 2000), p. 138.
23 Conversation with author.
24 Jeff Jacoby, *Washington Times*; Conservative Watch, *www.zmag.org.*
25 Interview with John Ashcroft, *Charisma*, December 1999.
26 Robert Parry, *Consortium News*, 11 October 2000.
27 Ibid.
28 *Denver Post*, 26 October 1992.
29 *Washington Times*, 31 December 1999.
30 'Pat Robertson, Road to Victory', 1991. *www.theocracywatch.org*; Don Lattin, 'Faith based welfare puzzles televangelist', *San Francisco Chronicle*, 22 February 2001. (From the book *Pat Robertson: The Most Dangerous Man in America?* by Rob Boston).
31 Prayer Breakfast at the Hyatt Hotel, Washington, 19 January 2001; Joe Conason, *New York Observer*, 12 February 2001.
32 Don Lattin, 'Faith based welfare puzzles televangelist', *San Francisco Chronicle*, 22 February 2001.

Chapter 5   The Question of Israel

1 *www.corkpsc.org.*
2 Ibid. See also Grace Halsell, 'The Clintons: American hostages in the holy land', *Washington Report*, January–February 1995. (The 'witness' here was Grace Halsell herself.)
3 Prayer Breakfast at the Israeli Embassy in Washington, May 2002.
4 Stan Crock, 'Bush, the Bible and Irak', *BusinessWeek*, 7 March 2003.
5 Ibid.
6 Jim Lobe, 'Evangelical Christians and the Sharon lobby', *Commentary*, 24 April 2002.
7 Ibid.
8 Ibid.
9 Ibid.
10 'Spinning dispensationalism', *Dubia Report*, 8 April 2002.
11 Donald Wagner, 'Evangelicals and Israel: theological roots of a political alliance', *Christian Century*, 4 November 1998.
12 'Meet the new Zionists', *The Guardian*, 28 October 2002.

13 Ibid.
14 William Cook, *Counter Punch*, 22 February 2002.
15 Christians for Israel USA, *www.christiansforisrael.org*.
16 Alison Mitchell, 'Israel winning broad support from U.S. right', *New York Times*, 21 April 2002; *www.commondreams.org*.
17 Letter to President Bush from evangelicals, 11 April 2002.
18 Ken Silverstein and Michael Sherer, *Mother Jones*, September/October 2002.
19 Gershom Gorenberg, 'Look who's in bed with the Christian right', *International Herald Tribune*, 14 October 2002.
20 Ibid.
21 Wagner, 'Evangelicals and Israel'.
22 Ibid.
23 National Religious Broadcasters Convention, Nashville, 10 February 2003; Dana Milbank, 'Bush links faith and agenda in speech to Broadcast group', *Washington Post*, 11 February 2003.
24 Ibid.
25 William Cook, *Counter Punch*, 22 February 2002.
26 Henri Tinck, 'Des missionnaires baptistes dans les fourgons de l'armée', *Le Monde*, 5 April 2003.
27 Reuters, 28 November 2001.

Chapter 6   Hawks and Doves

1 *www.soltam.com/soltam_systems/index.html*.
2 *www.centerforsecuritypolicy.org*.
3 Julian Borger, 'Washington hawks get power boost', *The Guardian*, 17 December 2001.
4 Conversation with author.
5 *www.jinsa.org/about/about.html*.
6 Ibid.
7 'The worst man in the worst place: Elliott Abrams put in charge of the Middle East in the US National Security Council', *As-Saffir* (Beirut), 4 December 2002.
8 Ibid.
9 Laila Al-Marayati, 'The biases of Elliott Abrams', *Counter Punch*, 16 December 2002.
10 David Com, 'Elliott Abrams. It's back!', *The Nation*, 2 July 2001.
11 Steven R. Weisman, 'Abrams back in capital fray at centre of Mideast battle', *New York Times*, 6 December 2002.
12 Ibid.

13 Matthew E. Berger, 'Elliott Abrams is Bush's new Mideast man', *Jewish Telegraphic Agency*, 13 December 2002.

14 Washington report on Middle East affairs, March 2000, pp.105–6; Allan C. Brownfeld book review of Israel Shahak and Norton Mezvinsky, *Jewish Fundamentalism in Israel* (London: Pluto Press, 1999).

15 James Besser, 'Ari Fleischer: Reform Lubavitch', *Baltimore Jewish Times*, 26 October 2001.

16 Ibid.

17 John R. Bolton, 'Kofi Annan's UN power grab', *Weekly Standard*, posted 1 November 1999.

18 'Kuwaiti Paper criticizes Syria: Assad's regime more criminal than Saddam's regime', MEMRI (Middle East Media Research Institute), special dispatch, 11 April 2003.

Chapter 7   The Middle East in Focus

1 Akiva Eldar, 'Perles of Wisdom for the Feithful', *Ha'aretz*, *www.israeleconomy.org/strat.html*.

2 Ibid.

3 Ibid.

4 Ibid.

5 Ibid.

6 Neil Mackay, 'Bush planned Iraq "regime change" before becoming President', *Sunday Herald*, 15 September 2002.

7 Ibid.

8 Lamis Andoni, 'In the service of empire', *Al-Ahram Weekly*, 12–18 December 2002.

9 Ibid.

10 Letter to President Clinton, 26 January 1998, *www.newamericancentury.org/iraqclintonletter.html*.

11 Committee for Peace and Security in the Gulf, open letter to the President, 19 February 1998, *www.centerforsecuritypolicy.org/index.jsp?section=paper&code=98-D_33at*.

12 Conversation with author.

13 Conversation with author.

14 'Netanyahu preached fascist war in US', *Executive Intelligence Review*, 29/16, 16 April 2002.

15 Ibid.

16 Ibid.

17 Uri Avnery, 'War now!', *Palestine Chronicle*, 7 September 2002.

18 Ben Lynfield, 'Israel sees opportunity in possible US strike on Iraq', *Christian Science Monitor*, 30 August 2002.

19 Bill Keller, 'The sunshine warrior', *New York Times Magazine*, 22 September 2002.

20 Conversation with author.

21 Conversation with author.

22 See John Gersham, 'Dreams of empire: eulogies for international law', *Counter Punch*, 29 March 2003.

23 John King, CNN, 27 September 2002.

24 Dana Milbank, *Washington Post*, 27 November 2002; Bill and Kathleen Christison, *Counter Punch*, 25 January 2003.

Chapter 8   The New Jerusalem?

1 See Jeffrey Steinberg, Anton Chaitkin and Scott Thompson, 'Dirty money schemes to steal election for Sharon', *Executive Intelligence Review*, 13 December 2002.

2 Yechiel Leiter, 'Hothouse for Hotheads', *Jerusalem Post*, 1 May 1994.

3 Steinberg, Chaitkin and Thompson, 'Dirty money'.

4 Ibid.

5 Ibid.

6 Ibid.

7 Ibid.

8 Thomas E. Ricks, 'Briefing depicted Saudis as enemies', *Washington Post*, 6 August 2002.

9 Mark Thompson, 'Inside the secret war council'. CNN, 19 August 2002, *www.cnn.com*.

Chapter 9   The New Arms Race

1 Seymour M. Hersh, 'Lunch with the chairman', *New Yorker*, 17 March 2003.

2 Ibid.

3 Ibid.

4 Ibid.

5 Ibid.

6 Ibid.

7 Ibid.

8 Ibid.

9   Jeff Koopersmith, 'Richard Perle: dead man walking', *American Politics Journal*, 27 March 2003.

10   Stephen Labaton, 'Pentagon adviser is stepping down', *New York Times*, 28 March 2003.

11   James Zogby, 'New questions about Feith', *Washington Watch*, 13 May 2001.

Chapter 10   Cheney and Company

1   Interview in 'This Week', ABC-TV, 30 July 2002.

2   Jason Leopold, 'Jason's lies about Halliburton and Iraq', *Counter Punch*, 19 March 2003.

3   Alex Berenson and Lowell Bergman, 'The Freedom of Information Center under Cheney: Halliburton Altered Policy on Accounting', *New York Times*, 22 May 2002.

4   Colum Lynch, 'Affiliates had $73 million in contracts', *Washington Post*, 23 June 2001.

5   Kenny Bruno and Jim Valette, 'Cheney and Halliburton: go where the oil is', *Third World Traveller*, *Multinational Monitor* magazine, May 2001.

6   Ken Silverstein, 'So you want to trade with a dictator', *Mother Jones*, May/June 1998.

7   Ibid.

8   Charles Pope, 'Contracts doled out to rebuild Iraq are questioned', *Seattle Post-Intelligencer*, 28 March 2003.

9   Ibid.

10   Pratap Chatterjee, 'The war on terrorism's gravy train', *CorpWatch*, 2 May 2002.

11   Jeff Gerth and Don Van Natta Jr, 'In tough times, a company finds profits in terror war', *New York Times*, 13 July 2002.

12   S. C. Gwynne, 'Did Dick Cheney sink Halliburton (and will it sink him)?', *Texas Monthly*, October 2002.

13   Ibid.

14   Berenson and Bergman, 'Under Cheney'.

15   Dana Milbank, 'For Cheney, tarnish from Halliburton firm's fall raises questions about Vice-Presidents' leadership there', *Washington Post*, 16 July 2002.

16   Ibid.

17   Knut Royce and Nathaniel Heller, 'Cheney led Halliburton to feast at Federal though State Department questioned deal with firm linked to Russian mob', www.apfn.org/enron/halliburton.htm.

18 Conversation with author.
19 Royce and Heller, 'Cheney led Halliburton'.

Chapter 11   A Corrupt Administration?

1 Robert L. Borosage, 'White must go', *The Nation*, 11 March 2002.
2 Ibid.
3 Ibid.
4 Jayson Blair, 'Ft. Hamilton utility deal with Enron is questioned', *New York Times*, 10 March 2002.
5 Sharon Theimer, 'Senators press army chief on Enron', Associated Press, 6 March 2002.
6 Ellen Nakashima, 'In midst of official trip to Seattle, Army Secretary and White closed on the sale of Aspen home. White used military jet for Colorado visit', *Washington Post*, 23 March 2002.
7 Joshua Green, 'The Gate-less community', *Washington Monthly*, July/August 2002.
8 Conversation with author.
9 Green, 'Gate-less community'.
10 *Washington Post*, July 2001.
11 Norman Mailer, 'Only in America', speech to the Commonwealth Club of California, 20 February 2003. Full text at *www. commonwealthclub.org/ archives/03/03–02mailer-speech.html*.
12 Eric Alterman, 'USA Oui! Bush Non!' *The Nation*, 10 February 2003.

Index